A Deaf Child
Listened

BOOKS BY THE SAME AUTHOR:

TOUCH OF LIGHT, *The Story of Louis Braille*
SIGMUND FREUD, *The World Within*
WITH THIS GIFT, *The Story of Edgar Cayce*
DAMIEN, THE LEPER PRIEST

Anne E. Neimark

A Deaf Child Listened

Thomas Gallaudet, Pioneer in American Education

WILLIAM MORROW AND COMPANY
NEW YORK 1983

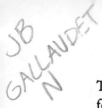

THE AUTHOR WISHES TO EXTEND SPECIAL THANKS for information and assistance to Winfield McChord, Jr., Executive Director, American School for the Deaf; Frank Asklar, Instructor, American School for the Deaf; Donna L. Chitwood, Media Relations, Gallaudet College.

Printed in the United States of America.

10 9 8 7 6 5 4 3 2

Library of Congress Cataloging in Publication Data
Neimark, Anne E. A deaf child listened.
Bibliography: p. Includes index. Summary: A biography of a man whose pioneering efforts in educating deaf children in the early part of the nineteenth century are still being felt today. 1. Gallaudet, T. H. (Thomas Hopkins), 1787–1851—Juvenile literature. 2. Teachers of the deaf—United States—Biography—Juvenile literature. [1. Gallaudet, T. H. (Thomas Hopkins), 1787–1851. 2. Teachers of the deaf] I. Title. HV2534.G3N44 1983   371.91'2'0924 [B] [92]   82-23942
ISBN 0-688-01719-3

To Edward Phillip Kaufman
—who teaches me another
language

"Silence more musical than any song."
Christina Rossetti

"The world is a sign, a way of speaking."
Muriel Rukeyser

Chapter
One

 Hartford's Main Street lay in silence in the hours before dawn. The slender, dark-haired boy slipped softly past Center Church, arms pressed flat against his sides. The year was 1802, and Thomas Gallaudet was fifteen years old. Around him, the air of the August night felt cool, distracting him from the fevered aching in his chest.

The town of Hartford, sharing honors as Connecticut state capital with New Haven, had been founded in 1635 by a great-great-great-grandfather of Thomas' mother. The Reverend Mr. Thomas Hooker had struck the first trail from Boston to the Connecticut River, leading a band of one hundred migrants with him. Thomas Gallaudet was named for his maternal grandfather, Thomas Hopkins, the sea captain who carried bricks and shingles across the seas from Holland to build the first brick house in Hartford. The mark of Thomas' family was carved into the very structure of the town. Thomas' father, Peter Wallace Gallaudet, was the grandson of French Huguenots. Tall and brawny, he'd opened a store in Hartford and, at the age of thirty-seven, gained respect for becoming a strict Bible-reader.

Thomas had neither the muscles of a sea captain nor of a rugged merchant. In 1802, he was the eldest of eight children. Small in stature and frail, he fit easily into the clothes of his brother Charles, who was four years younger and two inches taller. Climbing behind Charles over jutting hillsides and stone fences on the Connecticut terrain, Thomas was always aching for breath. His face would pale and his chest burn as if hot coals had tumbled down his throat. His eyes blurred, despite his eyeglasses, bought from the general store.

He'd been examined by Dr. Fuller on Main Street, the doctor pressing an ear against Thomas' chest so the sounds inside could be heard. Dr. Fuller didn't say much to Thomas' mother. The boy had a condition, he'd explained. If he kept eating hearty meals, he might well outgrow it.

But Thomas hadn't outgrown his condition. He could set forth in a wild dash with his brother or friends to prowl about the woolen mills for sight of the monthly wagonload of bobbins and spools. The mills would be filled with a smell of oil, and before long the oil fumes and the run across fields of lupine and wild geranium would have made Thomas ill and breathless. He'd stop, retreating from the laughter to the woods near the family house on Prospect Street. There, amid white dogwood and sugar maples, he'd sit against a broad, friendly trunk and begin his dreaming.

He wrote of the dreams in a secret journal that he hid in the attic bedroom where he and Charles slept. Even when he moved away from the house on Prospect Street, he

2

would continue a journal or diary. His youthful fancy, he said, was captured by the dreams of those aching and breathless hours beneath some venerable tree. His diary told of how he "used to delight to dwell upon what *might* be, and to conjure up such scenes of prosperity for myself and friends and all mankind."

Now Thomas walked from Main Street to the pitted dirt yard of the Jeremy Addams Tavern. By its door, stage-coaches loaded and left before dawn, clattering southward down Main Street, over a stone bridge, and onto the thirty-six-mile-long turnpike to New Haven. The Jeremy Addams served as inn, postal station, and meeting spot for business-men and town officials. Sneaking out of his house this night, Thomas had tiptoed past Center Church to wait in the sil-very shadows until the stagecoach admitted its passengers. He wanted to immerse himself in the black leather and wood of the carriage, to find reassurance in its bulk. For in the first week of September, he planned to be a passenger on that same stagecoach.

In June, he had graduated from Hartford Grammar School. His father announced to the family that business was good enough to send eldest son Thomas for examina-tions and entrance at Yale College in New Haven. The family had not always been so comfortable. Fifteen years earlier, when Thomas was born on December 10, 1787, Peter Wallace and Jane Hopkins Gallaudet were eking out a living in the city of Philadelphia. Only in 1800, after the Gallaudets settled in Hartford, did Peter Wallace begin to prosper, and success turn him in gratitude to the Congrega-tional Church.

Thomas was excited by the prospect of entering college,

3

by "what *might* be," as he wrote of his dreaming. Often, his father quoted from the Bible, citing a proverb of Solomon: "To know wisdom and instruction; to perceive the words of understanding." Could he know such things? Thomas had wondered of himself. In grammar school, he'd studied hard enough to win commendation from his teachers, reading by candle at night. He'd sought to make up for the frailty in his body and the meagerness of his height. Yale had loomed beyond his dreams like a quiet stronghold, and until the August night when he stood in shadow by the Jeremy Addams, he'd thought deliverance for him might be possible.

A lantern glow from the tavern seemed to Thomas like an ocher-colored eye, discovering him and watching. With fluttering breath, he leaned against the west wall of the building. The stagecoach stood by the front door, six horses already harnessed. Smells of hide and manure prickled his nostrils, and some lingering scent from the tavern kitchen seared his chest. He lurched toward an empty hitching post where a broken carriage wheel was propped and stooped down to touch the dry, splintery spokes. Behind him came the rustle of passengers emerging from the tavern doorway. Soon they'd hoist themselves into the coach and onto the backless benches. The driver would lift his whip, grunt a muffled command, and the thrusting horses would pull the coach in their wake—grinding toward Little River Bridge, the turnpike, and New Haven.

In two weeks, Thomas would feel the stagecoach vibrating under his own feet and see the dairy and poultry farms speckling the hills. His passage would be paid, his examinations scheduled at Yale; he would be starting his new life.

4

But he'd worried over whether he could "manage." Just that morning, he'd climbed several limbs of the Charter Oak, having crossed the Wyllys estate to the old, gnarly tree. Over a hundred years earlier, a hole in the oak had been the hiding place of the charter granted Connecticut by England. In 1687, a Sir Edmond Andros had come to Hartford as the representative of the Crown with the intention of dissolving the organizing charter. At a meeting in the Jeremy Addams, candles had been snuffed and the documents swept away from Andros to the safety of the tree that would become known as the Charter Oak.

So there Thomas had been, climbing higher and higher into the old tree, scanning the Wyllys estate for some view to stay indelible in his mind after he left Hartford for Yale. He could have dropped his diary down the same hole claimed for Connecticut's charter, but he didn't choose to leave everything behind. He knew he'd miss the sounds of home—of Charles' quill pen scratching out drawings in the attic or of William Edgar's somersaults on the landing. Reaching up, he had grabbed onto a higher limb, when suddenly his breath burned in his throat. Pains struck at his chest like dozens of nails. Gasping for air, he'd felt a familiar wetness beading his forehead, and he'd groaned over not even being able to climb a tree. How could he have imagined that his health might be any different at Yale?

The burning in Thomas' chest had lasted all day and night. Before dawn, it drove him out of bed and onto deserted Main Street, compelling him to find the stagecoach and try somehow to draw on its strength. Ten passengers, hatted and cloaked, were settled in the ebony depths of the coach. Sinking back into the darkness, Thomas was nearly out of the yard when he heard the driver shout to the innkeeper about a carriage wheel intended for repair in New Haven.

At the hitching post, Thomas bent down over the grimy wheel. He hadn't wanted to be seen, yet he needed something to do, some useful task or deed. Inhaling a tight, sharp breath, he reached forward and lifted the wheel. Calling out to the driver, his voice ragged, he stumbled heavily alongside the coach. Passengers stared down at him from their leather cushions and, in the lantern light falling from the tavern window, he saw the shadows of the wheel spokes spread in slashes at his feet.

Straining, Thomas sucked in more air and raised his face to the driver. Abruptly, from behind him, powerful arms arched over and wrenched the wheel from his grasp. Later, he carefully transcribed in his diary the words that the innkeeper barked at him. "You're much too short and puny," the man scolded. "An upping stone is what you'd need—like the ladies mount to their horses—to put yourself in square spitting distance of our driver."

"If only," Thomas wrote in a trembling but urgent script, "if only feelings could be discarded like boots, and a new set purchased."

New Haven Green stretched out broadly in sixteen acres. Its lush texture of land was bordered by homes, stores, and churches, displaying at center a pillared state house. On the west end of the Green was Yale College, three rectangular buildings ornamented by elm trees and manicured paths. Thomas found his way down one of the paths, inside a door to the administration building, and across a tiled corridor to President Timothy Dwight's office. There, beneath a framed sketch of Yale's first brick building on the Green and a printed roster of the first graduating class of 1718, he received a firm handshake of greeting.

Along with other freshman applicants, Thomas spent a full day at oral and written examinations in English, Greek, mathematics, and Latin. Afterwards, he waited tensely in Connecticut Hall to receive his scores. His eyeglasses clouded, and he kept cleaning them with a handkerchief before he realized that the clouding was actually in his eyes. At last, President Dwight opened the door of the admitting office and gestured to him as he waited in the corridor. The paper pressed into his hands was grained like the bleached linen paper sheets sized at the mill in East Hartford. He squinted down at the first paragraph, reading in mid-sentence, ". . . acceptance of Thomas Hopkins Gallaudet with sophomore standing in the program of Yale College, New Haven, Connecticut."

Sophomore? *A sophomore?* Thomas was suddenly dizzy. He would recall feeling lost in one of his dreams. Not until the next morning's chapel service did he truly believe what he'd read. His test scores had allowed him to skip freshman year at Yale and to begin his studies as a second-year student.

College became for Thomas a place of books and comforting routine. The sole exception lay in Yale's dreaded *Book of Rules and Customs.* He was forbidden, he learned, to explore past any two-mile point from campus without permission from President Dwight. He could not wear his hat in the front yard of any faculty member's house or "within

7

ten rods of the person of the president, eight rods of the professor, and five rods of the tutor." He would be fined a halfpenny, sixpence, or a shilling for absences from his chamber during study hours or for such wanton acts of misbehavior as tardiness, picking open a lock, or jumping from a window to avoid detection.

Five or six times, he paid a halfpenny for oversleeping. His being late to Roman history class was because he attended the long, nightly practice sessions of the debating teams. Debates were the most popular sport at Yale, far outdistancing football, tobogganing, or skating. Fierce weekly skirmishes took place between the small debating teams to ferret out students who qualified for the larger groups. Eager to play this game of logic, Thomas researched some of the subjects under debate. His first notecards were for the question: "Ought the Dictates of Conscience Invariably Be Followed?" The next week, he found morality turning to philosophy and science with the question, "Have Brutes Reason?"

One evening, as Thomas sat in the rear of a classroom, a debate floundered through an opening argument. By the time of final rebutting, the moderator had called on Thomas Gallaudet to take the chair. Bolting forward, he'd nodded at his tall, ruddy-faced opponent, a freshman named Gardiner Spring, and tremulously he began rebuttal.

He quickly found himself relaxing as he began to play with the patterns made by words built upon words. He'd watched premise become argument, which he now designed into counteroffense. Opposing Gardiner Spring's defense of slavery in the United States, Thomas scored the winning points for his team. Hands slapped him on the back and a member of the Brothers of Unity, one of Yale's largest debating groups, asked the spelling of his name.

The Brothers of Unity invited Thomas to join their ranks. In a matter of months, he was a star debater. He composed a book of sample questions and arguments for the team, writing of "aiming at truth and truth alone, far from the noise of proud Ambition's bustle and alarm." He'd not forgotten Solomon's proverb, quoted by his father at family suppers in Hartford. To comprehend the words of understanding, to know wisdom and instruction could well have been a motto of the Brothers of Unity.

On vacations home from Yale, Thomas was given a grand welcome by parents, sisters, and brothers. Always, he would arrive somewhat thin and pale at the Jeremy Addams, along with a few fellow passengers who'd disembarked from ships at Long Island Sound. But on the walk down Main Street, he'd assure his mother that his breathing had improved, that his eyesight was clear, and that he would grow strong and fat on her corn cakes and bread.

Three years slipped by in the cycle of periods of study at Yale and restful sojourns at home. Thomas was voted president of the Brothers of Unity and earned top grades in geometry, Roman history, Greek, Latin, and English. Then it was June, 1805. The Green burst out in cowslips and a laurel festival was held beside the state house. Yale's September graduating class would contain forty-two students. Its youngest member—Thomas Hopkins Gallaudet of Hartford—was one of six students whose grades merited the honor of an oration. He was also tied, rumor had it, with Gardiner Spring in the faculty choice of class valedictorian.

The halls of the college were astir with speculation.

Thomas tried not to think or dream about the valedictorian award. He tried, instead, to remember what he'd written in his debate book of Ambition, of all its "bustle and alarm." When he was summoned, on a Thursday, to President Dwight's office, he went without a word. He was congratulated for his achievements and advised to channel his interests into the fields of business or education. President Dwight informed him that he'd been singled out of his senior class for an additional graduation honor beyond the assigned oration.

Thomas' heart was knocking in his chest and he ached for air. He wondered if he'd truly been elected class valedictorian.

Tilting back in his chair, President Dwight spoke again. Thomas, he said, was to be Latin Salutatorian in the discourse, "Timophanes, or the Tyrant of Corinth." He must be deeply and justly pleased. However—and unfortunately —he had not been chosen class valedictorian. The vote, said President Dwight, had gone to Gardiner Spring. But the decision was certainly not because Gardiner Spring was the best qualified student. "No, no," said President Dwight. "Not at all."

Stillness enveloped the room. Politely, Thomas waited for whatever words would come next.

President Dwight cleared his throat. At graduation, he said, portions of the audience would be seated far in the back rows . . . and since Thomas was merely five feet, six inches tall and not very robust . . . and since Gardiner Spring was three or four inches taller . . . well, the faculty had voted Gardiner Spring a more suitable choice. Surely Thomas could understand?

Thomas nodded. Yet understanding, he would find, was sometimes quite difficult. He thanked President Dwight for whatever honors had been awarded him and let himself out the door. A chapel clock chimed across the Green, and he walked down the corridors of Connecticut Hall listening to the muted, persistent sounds. His shadow spiraled above him on the wall. Perhaps, he would tell his diary, he should have suggested an *upping stone* for the ceremony of graduation. Then he could have been seen easily by the audience sitting far in the back rows. But, he wrote, he must rid himself of such "a melancholy of mind." He was nineteen years old and already he was graduating from Yale College. It was only Ambition, puny Ambition, that tempted or taunted him—not the better urgings from any of his dreams.

Chapter
Two

In spring, the backwoods of eastern Kentucky were a maze of trees and flowering vines. April rains made ruts and gulleys fill with a brownish sludge, which would bake dry in the summer heat. Thomas rode his dappled mare over the roads that had been marked on maps in his canvas sacks. Bulging from the canvas were the goods he was selling in rural Kentucky and Ohio—tinware, brass buttons, steel pins and needles, ribbons, swatches of wool, gun parts, and painted clocks.

The goods were manufactured in Connecticut and bought wholesale by a New York firm that hired him to be a salesman. At first, Thomas couldn't imagine himself a peddler, living from hand to mouth, leaving civilization behind. But the idea of fresh air and exercise seemed a saving grace. Five years had passed since Yale, and though he'd held two jobs that had promised to advance him, in Hartford and New Haven, his health could be summed up in a word written bitterly in his diary—*rursus,* Latin for "backwards."

The law firm that Thomas joined after graduation was owned by the Honorable Chauncey Goodrich of Hartford; his supervisor was the chief justice of Connecticut. He'd learned to write briefs and handle minor legal disputes, yet at the end of one year he was so breathless in the choking layers of pipe smoke that he had to resign. For nearly eighteen months, he'd recuperated at home. He studied English literature and spoke at local seminars on law and education. He wrote articles for the Hartford *Courant* and for *The Children's Magazine,* the only publication for children in America. He was able to keep up a cheerful front but, in private, melancholy doubts plagued him anew. The pages of his diary revealed his "torments of mind," and his vow that if he were restored to health and strength, he'd find some worthy way to live his life.

When Thomas received an offer for tutoring at Yale, with the privilege of earning a master's degree, he was well enough to make the arduous journey by stagecoach to Connecticut Hall. His students liked him, dubbing him "the little tutor who knows the answers." He remained two years at the post, and if his breath faltered in his throat or his eyes failed, no one was the wiser. Only once did the strain show on him, after he tried to dull the ache in his chest by drinking too much wine at a faculty social gathering and had to be led to his quarters. Never again did he allow himself to lose control in such fashion, to be "too irritable" over his health. He was so stung by the incident that he spent a weekend at Center Church in Hartford, where his father was now treasurer, talking with the pastor about his "pigheaded foolishness."

An unrelenting siege of breathlessness forced Thomas to

relinquish Yale and his latest dreams of "what *might* be." The job of itinerant salesman came as a welcome escape. Each day he rode on horseback into the back country, calling on farms and cabins along his route. Families seated him at roughhewn tables, piling his plate with deer stew or mutton, carrot cake or preserved fruit. After a meal, he'd open his canvas sack and, as if offering a carnival grab bag, pull out the enticing objects of tin, steel, brass, and ribbon. The children of the family crouched beside him in patched knickers or faded dresses, staring saucer-eyed at the treasures he brought forth. Housewives would wipe red-knuckled hands on aprons and gaze wistfully at a new iron hearth kettle or an Eli Terry clock.

Thomas carried in his pocket a tiny notebook, his Kentucky and Ohio Journal, where he jotted down mileage and lodging. "Arrived in Lexington," he wrote on February 2, 1811. "Distance from Frankfort, 22 miles. Left Lexington and arrived next day at Handford. May my present journey be the means of restoring me to complete health so that I may hereafter lead a more active and zealous life." One entry was made while his horse drank at a forest pond amid a haze of crane flies. Stronger but tired, Thomas addressed his words to God: "Leave me not, neither forsake me," he wrote. "How can I complain at the little inconveniences?"

By the end of the first selling season, he added up his receipts to find that the company had profited from his territory, but he had earned little. The reasons were the "bonuses" he dispensed with sales, paid for out of his own pocket. He couldn't resist the flush of joy on a child's face when, sack strapped on his horse for leave-taking, he clipped a ribbon bow onto a pinafore or a jackknife over a belt. He never failed to notice the rigors of farm life. He'd

14

seen the hours spent at churning and spinning or at the plow, axe, and scythe. He'd slept in cabins without books or pictures. If he couldn't leave behind seeds of learning to germinate in children's minds, he could still tender his pretty ribbons and shiny trinkets.

One October evening in Millerstown, Ohio, Thomas stayed overnight with a farm family, the four children plumping up their feather bed for the "Mister" and unrolling a floor mat for themselves. After he'd sold the parents a packet of needles and a shelf clock with an enameled dial, he'd gone outside with the children to see the newborn piglets in their wire pen. The sun had dipped behind the sloped roof of the barn, striating the yard with amber light, and Thomas kept blinking behind his eyeglasses until trees, barn, and yard were clearly defined.

Near the path to the pigpen, he noticed two miniature gravestones. They were, the children told him, for a thirteen-year-old sister who'd died of consumption and a seven-year-old brother killed by lightning. As the two girls and two boys zigzagged along the path, Thomas asked if they ever read from books. They shook their heads, telling him that the town schoolmarm had disappeared and a newly hired teacher was yet to arrive. And when Thomas had mentioned James Madison, there was not even a spark of recognition. So, while the piglets were admired for their pink underbellies and corkscrew tails, he began to talk of Washington, Adams, Jefferson, and Madison. In the cabin, he drew a map of the seventeen states of the union and described an article on presidents that he'd composed for *The Children's Magazine.* That evening, he wrote in his journal that the young sister and brother who'd died on the farm and the four children left behind were most likely starved for knowledge of the world beyond Millerstown. The wares in his sack were not enough education. "Does God frown," he wondered of his peddling, "upon my intended business?" How could it be sufficient to dispense only a dozen needles and a shelf clock, a ribbon or a brass button, in the shingled cabin?

Settling down that night on the feather bed, Thomas listened to the clicking pendulum of the clock with the enameled dial. *Hur-ry up,* it seemed to be saying, and he remembered his vow to make his life worthy. So far, he decided, the vow was unfulfilled. He'd signed a second contract to sell in the coming season, but ledgers and numbers were not the answer for him. If his health kept improving, might he not rekindle his dreams?

Beneath the steady rhythm of the clock, Thomas could hear the sleep sounds of the four children curled onto the blanketed mat. Before his horse was saddled in the morning, he would tell them Matthew's parable of the treasure, which contained another of his father's favorite quotations. "The kingdom of heaven," said the parable, "is like unto a merchant man seeking goodly pearls; who, when he had found one pearl of great price, went and sold all that he had, and bought it."

Seeking the pearl, Thomas mused sleepily, was what he must do. He would not let himself stop searching. Since childhood, he'd focused on the *wrongs* inside his own body. Now he must pursue, both inside himself and out, what seemed most *right*—giving all that he had of his strength to sustain it.

A year of blank pages collected in Thomas' journal.

Then, in a rush of script, came a journal entry dated Sunday, January 12, 1812—Andover, Massachusetts: "I joined the day before yesterday the divinity college in this place, and this morning took up residence within its walls."

At the age of twenty-six, he was going to study to be a minister. The words of Scripture filled him with a sense of truth. He'd always felt drawn toward the written or spoken word. At Yale, he'd spun words into arguments for debate or mined them for his sessions with the students he tutored. In Hartford, at the Honorable Chauncey Goodrich's firm, he'd built words into legal pyramids of fact and precedent. Words had sung, drifted, or marched through his mind. And having seen the children of the farms and woods, he'd longed to speak to them of the valor of the human spirit and of the sovereignty of God.

For two years, he studied at Andover College. By September, 1814, when he earned his diploma, several parishes had sent him offers. He decided, however, not to count on his better health for any permanent post but to preach as a visiting minister. To one church in Portsmouth, New Hampshire, he sent a letter of regret, informing the officer and new congressman, Daniel Webster, that he could not accept the North Parish pulpit. He did not mince words about his reasons. "My eyes and lungs are both weak," he said.

Through the following winter and spring, Thomas preached at churches in Connecticut, New Hampshire, and Massachusetts. He moved back to Hartford on weekdays, the number of his brothers and sisters having grown to nine. William Edgar had followed in his footsteps to Yale but planned to become a doctor. Charles, whose etchings had once been scattered across their attic room, was working in town as an engraver, and his sister Ann was to marry.

On a warm day in early summer, Thomas walked down Main Street in Hartford, pausing in the dimness of the Jeremy Addams for a glass of water and circling past the millinery shop with its window full of whalebone bonnets on stands. On Prospect Street, he unbuttoned his waistcoat and removed his hat. Trees splayed their branches into arches of brown and green, and squirrels were darting across picket fences. At the front path to the family house, Thomas felt weary. The shade of the small wooden porch tempted him, and he sat down on the steps and balanced his hat on one knee.

A cardinal soared from the porch roof, a flash of brilliant red, and then the quiet of the afternoon was broken by a burst of laughter. Turning toward the left end of the house, Thomas saw a group of children in a boisterous game of tag. Some of his younger sisters and brothers were at the heels of a boy in checkered britches. The children waved at Thomas and raced on, whooping like buccaneers. Soon the boy in the checkered britches was caught and stood, blindfolded, in a circle of his former chasers. Tottering forward, he was to tag the next object of sport.

All at once, at the edge of the lawn, Thomas noticed a little girl who had not taken part in the play. She looked about eight or nine years of age and was neatly dressed in a pink pinafore. A blankness in her face arrested Thomas' interest. He saw the child stare at the commotion around her. She didn't appear ill. Why hadn't one of the children asked her to join the game?

He called out to his brother Teddy. As the nine-year-old hopped onto the steps, face aflame, he was questioned about the little girl in the ruffled pink dress. Oh! Teddy said, she was Alice from down the street. Dr. Cogswell's daughter. She was deaf. Deaf and dumb. She couldn't hear anything or talk. She didn't know she was Alice.

Teddy sped away to the clamoring children, and Thomas walked slowly across the lawn toward Alice Cogswell. Under a tree, he bent down to pluck a tiny violet and offer it to the child. She sniffed at the flower warily but let Thomas take her hand, and together they walked to the porch and sat on the wooden steps. Rubbing the flower over her eyelids, Alice finally held it against her nose.

Deafness, in the 1800s, meant a life of hopelessness and uselessness. The winter before, while in Boston to preach, Thomas had rescued a deaf-mute boy from a grimy alley. Two dock workers had clapped their hands over the boy's ears and mocked him with guttural sounds. Now, Thomas glanced at the child who sat so quietly at his side. Her blond hair fell in ringlets to her shoulders. She didn't seem afflicted—but then, why should she? Deafness was not a crippled leg or missing arm. It didn't show. Who would have presumed that Dr. Cogswell's young daughter lived without words in a silent prison?

"You don't even know that your name is Alice," Thomas said aloud.

Putting his hat on Alice Cogswell's head, he smiled at her. An idea was taking root in his mind. He reached to pick up a stray stick from beneath the steps and drew the letters H A T in the sandy dirt. With the word completed, he retrieved his top hat and positioned it directly above the printed letters. A beginning, he asked himself, or a wasted, presumptuous act?

Alice giggled, a thin, high sound, and touched the tiny

petals of the violet. She waved the flower in the air and dropped it into a pocket of Thomas' waistcoat.

Once more he smiled at the child. Catching her eye, he pointed straight at the hat. Then he pointed to the stick-drawn word. Deliberately, he retraced the *H A T* with the stick. He pointed back to his hat.

This time Alice Cogswell tapped her shoes on the steps and wiggled her fingers. She must have thought, Thomas later wrote, that they both were playing a game. First he would do a trick, then so would she. How could teaching truly begin?

For more than an hour, Thomas patiently pulled Alice's attention to the indented letters and to his gray top hat. Her eyes showed no dawning of a connection between the design made by the stick and the object worn on the head. Teddy ran by with a neighborhood dog. He yelled that Alice didn't know things had names, that her father had tried teaching her.

By late afternoon, Thomas Gallaudet and Alice Cogswell were fast friends. Having younger sisters and brothers had given Thomas a feeling of ease among children. And his own childhood, where he, too, had stood apart, spurred an instant kinship with this child who could not hear.

He would never know the exact moment when comprehension was born in Alice Cogswell. If she wondered why he kept touching his hat and pointing and tracing fingers over the dirt—while she jumped and wiggled and tossed stones and tugged her hair—her wondering and her delight with Thomas must at last have let a door swing open just far enough for her to see the link between the *H A T* and the unnamed object that the smiling man put on his head.

Alice suddenly grabbed the top hat to clamp it down, lop-sided, over her curls. She pointed to the word made by Thomas, eagerly tapped his hat, and jumped off the steps in excitement. *H A T* and *hat?* The link had been made. She waited.

Leaping to the ground, Thomas swung the child into his arms. His weariness was gone. What an incredible day! How had this happened? He heard Alice's high-pitched giggle and he laughed in return. The hat toppled, spilling into a flower bed, and Alice plunged after it, pointing a finger directly at the word in the dirt. *Correct!* Thomas wanted to shout.

Several houses away, a carriage rolled into a pebbled driveway, wheels clattering, horses snorting. Thomas recognized Dr. Mason Cogswell, and he turned Alice to-ward the sounds, watching her face light up at the sight of her father. A yank on Thomas' arm said that she wanted him to come with her, but then she stopped and looked quizzi-cally at her new friend. She lunged for the stick and dragged Thomas onto the patch of dirt. Frantically, she pushed the stick into his hands and began thumping her fists on her own shoulders. *Me? Me? Me?* she seemed to be saying.

Again Thomas smiled. He saw Dr. Cogswell waving to him and to Alice, but he knelt down to smooth out a clear place in the sandy dirt. With the stick moving in his fingers like the most magical of wands, he started to write a large letter *A,* the very first letter of Alice Cogswell's name.

Chapter
Three

 In Dr. Mason Cogswell's study, Thomas was surrounded by a profusion of books. One wall of shelves was filled with medical texts, another with historical volumes, two with encyclopedias and monographs on philosophy, religion, and science. Books were stacked like pillars on a desk and tables. After Thomas had been fed buttered biscuits by Mrs. Cogswell and Alice persuaded by her mother's kisses and gestures to lie down for a nap, Dr. Cogswell had thrown an arm around Thomas' shoulders and swept him into the study.

The doctor still seemed unable to believe what had occurred. He adored his daughter—that Thomas could see—and spoke of the scarlet fever that had robbed her of her hearing at age two. Any words Alice had known slowly ebbed from her consciousness. The sounds she made grew garbled, a torrent of grunts or a high wailing cry. By the time she was four, she was judged a deaf-mute, a "dummy" —unable to hear or speak and thought incapable of understanding, a freak to be penned up or discarded in an asylum.

Dr. Cogswell had never accepted the judgment on his daughter. He didn't believe she was mentally impaired. He was certain that intelligence lived within the child, even if it lived under lock and key. In his medical texts, he researched early nineteenth-century theories on deafness, studying diagrams of ear dissections and of the three interior areas of the ear—the opening, or meatus, the middle ear, and the shell-shaped cochlea, or inner ear. Italian scientist Dominico Cotugno had discovered that the cochlea was an important center of hearing and was filled with fluid rather than air. Alice's scarlet fever had probably destroyed nerve fibers in the cochlea or in the main auditory nerve that transmitted sound impulses to the brain. No cure for deafness was known, and Dr. Cogswell turned to his history books to read whatever he could of the deaf.

He learned, to his sorrow, that many ancient cultures had killed their deaf offspring. Athenians and Spartans left them to die on mountaintops, and Romans abandoned them at the base of statues to be torn to pieces by dogs. In the Middle Ages, physicians would try to cure deaf-mutes with futile eardrum punctures or tongue slicings. Not until the sixteenth century did Spaniards Ponce de León and Juan Pablo Bonet teach several deaf sons of wealthy families to read, write, and even utter recognizable words. Yet three hundred years later, a mere handful of schools in Europe bothered to train the "dummies," and in America deaf education did not exist.

Thomas listened to Dr. Cogswell speak of deafness and of nine-year-old Alice trapped in her soundless prison. Being deaf, Thomas learned, brought a greater penalty than being blind. Deaf-born children, receiving no words, couldn't learn to think in organized language. The panorama of the world passed before them without much reassurance. Ordinary sounds—insects buzzing, rain thrumming, the pleasant drone of far-away voices—might tell the hearing that all was safe. But for the deaf, there was only the terror of a silence without end.

The Cogswells had hesitated to send Alice across the seas to one of the few European schools. Her helplessness frightened them, and they had tried without success to educate her themselves. But now, Dr. Cogswell exclaimed, Alice wouldn't need to go away. She wouldn't have to live in ignorance or be a freak. In one afternoon, young Mr. Gallaudet had wrought some kind of miracle. He would continue to help Alice, wouldn't he? He would become her teacher?

By supper, Thomas left the study of the Cogswell house with the questions posed by Dr. Cogswell and with two French volumes entitled *Théorie des Signes.* The set of books, written by a priest, the Abbé Sicard, had been ordered from Paris, from the Royal Institution for the Deaf and Dumb. In his attic bedroom, Thomas leafed through printed drawings and Dr. Cogswell's English translations of a one-handed manual alphabet and of hand gestures, or signs, representing words, phrases, or sentences. The alphabet letter *A,* Thomas saw, was formed by simply folding down the fingers onto the top of the palm and laying the unfolded thumb against the side of the index finger. Other alphabet letters each required particular positions of fingers and hand.

Some of the signs created an image, a pantomime, of the

intended word. The sign for *baby* was made by placing and rocking the right hand in the crook of the left arm. Many signs, however, were less obvious. The word *lonely* was signed by drawing the right index finger down across the lips, the palm facing left. And since pointing could readily indicate *I, you, he, she,* or *us,* this language of gestures did not provide for pronouns or articles. It also changed some of the familiar word order of English; noun subjects were given emphasis over adjectives, as in *girl pretty* instead of *pretty girl.*

Deaf children, Dr. Cogswell had told Thomas, roamed the alleys of Europe like animals. Those fortunate enough to be schooled were taught by one of two methods: an oral method, which trained people to watch or "read" lips and parrot some words; and the silent or natural method, based on the use of sign language instead of vocalized speech. The first method could only help the more skillful, while the second could enable anyone who knew the signs to communicate. Asylum schools hotly defended one system or the other, with England and Scotland on the oral side, and France promoting the silent gestures.

Thomas recalled the children of the Kentucky and Ohio farms who were growing to adulthood without books. But those children could *hear* the collected wisdom and stories of others. Alice Cogswell could not hear a sound. For her, newborn piglets did not squeal and shelf clocks didn't tick. The morning after talking to Dr. Cogswell, Thomas appeared at the Cogswell door and took Alice down Prospect Street. Exuberant, the child raced from object to object, skimming them with her fingertips and looking to Thomas for the words. He wrote large letters into a notebook, and

25

having already memorized the Abbé Sicard's manual alphabet, he spelled each word for Alice with his fingers. Did she understand? Later—tomorrow—he would begin teaching her signs and the one-handed letters. Teach her. Teacher. Yes, that's what he would agree to do and be. Weekends would see him in the pulpits of churches in New England. On weekdays, he would return to teach Alice Cogswell a language spoken by hand and not by mouth.

Soon, Thomas' younger sisters and brothers were trouping behind teacher and student, practicing the signs and finger alphabet and applauding Alice for mastering words. Her occasional tears of frustration at making mistakes were wiped away by the other children. She learned almost twenty words a day, each word urging her further through the door and beyond the wall that had kept her separate. Passersby stopped to watch the slight, eldest son of Peter Gallaudet lead the small band that etched pictures in midair like mimes upon a stage. To indicate the word *boy,* fingers of hands grasped imaginary hat brims. To say *girl,* thumbs on closed hands traced pretend bonnet strings from cheek to chin.

In April of 1815, Thomas was asked to speak at an evening meeting of ten merchants and educators in Dr. Mason Cogswell's parlor. Alice had advanced so rapidly that her father wanted the young minister to describe his teaching. A census of New England, said Dr. Cogswell, showed eighty-four deaf-mutes in Connecticut alone; thousands more from across the country were, if not totally deaf, hearing-impaired. The United States was to be the land of opportunity, yet only one public institution had been established—an asylum for the insane. Shouldn't there be schools for unfortunate children? Might not Thomas inspire the men in the parlor to found such a school? If a little girl like Alice could be educated, how many other girls and boys, or deaf adults for that matter, were capable of being taught?

Thomas stood in the hazy kerosene warmth of the Cogswell parlor before a semicircle of chairs and a polite but skeptical audience. Hands rested on knees or in laps, hands that were accustomed to ordinary use. Thomas must have wondered how he would convince these men of Hartford that a deaf child's hands might create words by shape. He'd learned that the deaf did not have to be ignorant or mute. Alice's fingers could speak in a silent language of nouns, verbs, and adjectives that even, by means of a specific sign, put sentences in past, present, or future tense. Lifting a leather Bible from the mantle, he referred to the Gospel of Saint John. "In the beginning was the Word," he said.

Through the evening, Thomas explained to his audience that God's Word must be made available to all His flock, that a school for the deaf would be a just and humane undertaking. At nine o'clock, an interruption came from a sleepy Alice in flannel nightgown and cotton slippers. Carried into the parlor by her father, the child sat on a rug by the fireplace. Thomas stooped beside her and tapped her hands. Gently, his own fingers asked his student to tell the ten gentlemen of Hartford what she felt about learning words.

Shyly, she smiled. From the edge of the rug, Alice's right hand rose, opening like a flower on its stem, and she swayed toward the music of her fingers. The little finger of her right hand touched her chest to indicate herself, and then her index finger, hand palm up, made a clockwise circle. She tapped her forehead and crooked and uncrooked her

27

fingers. Finally, after folding her fingers and curling her thumb beneath the first joint of her middle and index finger, Alice lifted her index finger and placed her hand in front of her forehead.

Thomas kissed the top of her head and turned to the men to translate the child's signing. *I always want—understand,* Alice Cogswell had said.

A unanimous vote was taken that evening among the ten merchants and educators. The men agreed to try to collect enough money to send an emissary to Europe to study the available methods of teaching the deaf. If more funds were collected, the first school in America for deaf students might be opened in Hartford. The town, boasted one merchant, contained the first stone state house in the country. Why shouldn't it be the site of another noteworthy first?

Thomas shook hands with each of the men. As he was leaving the Cogswell parlor, however, he stopped suddenly to clap his hands together in two sharp bursts of sound. Startled, the men looked at him. Clapping again, Thomas remarked that such a hand motion was not only a means of expressing approval or commanding respect. Two claps of the hands, he said, was French—and now American—sign language for the word *school.*

"Clap with me," Thomas invited the men. And echoing behind him, slow and awkward at first but soon growing firm, came a long series of double hand claps in behalf of the deaf.

By noon the next day, an impressive sum of money had been deposited in the Bank of Hartford. Some of the town's citizens, leaning in doorways of shops or convening at the Jeremy Addams, scoffed at the notion that deaf-mutes deserved any investment of time or capital. Yet others had seen little Alice Cogswell writing alphabet letters with the Reverend Mr. Gallaudet and were amazed at the child's development. Alice had been a sad and hopeless outcast. Now she jumped and played and could read and write words. If deafness only impaired the hearing and not the brain . . . why, investing in a Hartford school for the deaf would be a charitable act.

Thomas was not prepared for the outpouring of funds that followed his speech in the Cogswell parlor. Nor was he prepared for the proposition almost immediately offered him. The contributing citizens requested that Thomas himself be the emissary to Europe. They also wanted him to become principal and minister of any school for the deaf that would open in Hartford. He could live, even preach, in England or France until he was ready to bring what he'd learned back home.

No one, Thomas wrote in his diary, had mentioned his health. What if he couldn't complete a sojourn in Europe? What if he were a disappointment? But he wasn't able to talk himself into a hasty refusal. For reasons he could not fathom, he sensed that he might, for now, count on his strength rather than his frailty, on his being well rather than ill.

He asked for one week to submit his reply. In the meantime, he and Dr. Cogswell rode by wagon to Glastonbury, ten miles from Hartford. There, according to the Connecticut census, lived an eight-year-old deaf and blind girl whom Thomas wanted to meet. Her name was Julia Brace, and she had lost both sight and hearing during a severe case of typhus.

In her parents' farmhouse, Thomas shook hands with the

dark-haired child. She was, said her mother, a good-hearted little girl but most sorely afflicted. Beset by fits of temper, Julia would throw herself on the floor and scream out the only words she recalled hearing—the foul swearing of an old sea captain who'd fished with her before the typhus.

Thomas found it difficult to think of the girl screaming and swearing on the floor. She seemed well behaved. But then, she had to exist in both darkness *and* silence. Told that Julia had developed an extraordinary sense of smell and could match possessions with their owners, Thomas and Mason Cogswell slid their brass pocket watches into the child's hands.

Julia's face was instantly aglow. Sniffing strongly, she rubbed each watch under her nose, then grunted for them to be held by an older sister. Her arms flung outward toward the two strange men, she fastened onto their hands and sniffed carefully at palms and fingers. When the watches were again given to her by her sister, she was unaware that Thomas and Dr. Cogswell had been asked to change their positions in the room.

Julia staggered forward in a stiff, flatfooted gait. Her dress dragged on the floor and her eyes stared sightlessly ahead, but in a few moments she bumped into Thomas. Grinning, she grabbed at his hand and rubbed it under her nose. Half-gurgling, half-laughing, an oath escaping her lips like an exclamation of triumph, she sniffed again at the watches and dropped the one belonging to Thomas into his waistcoat pocket.

"She's so intelligent!" Thomas later told Mason Cogswell. "She belongs in a school with Alice. A school for the deaf." If Julia had tantrums, it was because she needed to

30

be taught a proper language. Swear words could be replaced by what her hands would teach her to say.

On May 25, 1815, in the harbor of New York City, Thomas stood by the deck rail of the small sailing ship *Mexico.* He waved down to his family, to Dr. Cogswell and Alice, and to nearly a hundred Hartford citizens who'd gathered on the wharf. In his pocket was a passport to Liverpool, England, signed by Secretary of State James Monroe. In his luggage in his sleeping quarters, along with the two volumes of *Théorie des Signes* by the Abbé Sicard and the reference letters written for him by the governor of Connecticut and a professor at Princeton, was a crisp new diary. The opening entry, dated a month before, on the morning of April 20, said: "I informed Dr. Mason F. Cogswell . . . of my willingness to undertake the employment of instructing the deaf in my own country."

Thomas had signed his name to the ship's passenger list and had been introduced to the man behind him in line, the well-known author Washington Irving. The two travelers agreed to meet for dinner. Now, only moments from the *Mexico*'s casting off, Thomas looked out on the expanse of blue water and back toward the tumult of merchants, sailors, families, and townspeople on shore. Though he did not record his thoughts of that moment, he'd wondered in the past month where he would find the true frontier of deafness—where the path of revelation might lie. Would he discover it in England, where deaf-mute children were taught by the oral system? Or was it in France, where the language of the deaf could flow swiftly through the fingers? Must a choice between the two methods be made?

What was most possible, Thomas may have thought as the

31

clang of the ship's bell sounded against his ears, was that the United States of America would pioneer its own treatment of deafness—as Thomas' ancestor Thomas Hooker had staked out a pioneering trail from Boston to the Connecticut River—forging into uncharted territory because of the need for change.

Chapter
Four

 The Committee of Subscribers at the Asylum for the Deaf and Dumb was resplendent in velvet cloaks and white ruffles. Outside, in congested London, carriages bearing advertisements for soap or bread clattered down cobbled streets. Overhead, birds veered toward the river Thames. Thomas had been careful to allow enough time for the walk from the hotel to the Kent Road asylum. This day, the subscribers were to choose some of London's shabbier deaf children for whom they would pay tuition. Boys and girls in frayed knickers and dresses clustered in the entryway and soon shuffled up two flights of stairs, holding tickets penciled by parents or sponsors that gave brief accounts of each claim on charity.

In the conference room, Thomas nodded hello to Dr. Watson, principal of the asylum, and to Rev. John Townshend, head of the Committee of Subscribers. The return nods were curt acknowledgements of his presence, no more. Sitting at a table, he added up the days since he'd left home. A month at sea. Over a month in London. And still nothing had been accomplished. Sign language was hardly discussed in the British Isles, and oral methods were not revealed to him.

Since the mid-1700s, the oral instruction of deaf-mutes in England had been controlled by a family named Braid-wood. All instructors and board members of the asylum were required to pledge a bond of £1000 against divulging any Braidwood methods of teaching. No one had dared invade or challenge the Braidwood regime, and officials at the Kent Road asylum weren't particularly happy to see Thomas—for he wanted knowledge that was secret. Dr. Watson and Mr. Townshend became quite practiced at avoiding him, and Dr. Watson didn't even arrange a preliminary introduction until the twenty-sixth of July. A "sad monopoly on the resources of charity," Thomas wrote of the Braidwoods' ambition.

He recorded that first interview in detail in his diary. He'd explained to Dr. Watson that he and his American backers simply sought to help the unfortunate deaf in their own country. "Nothing but the most intense confidence in the liberal and generous spirit of British Public Institutions of Charity," he said, "would have induced me to leave my native home. . . ." Yet Dr. Watson was not to be swayed by the urgency or compassion in Thomas' mission. "You might as well make experiments upon the deaf and dumb in the United States," said the principal, "as to try to learn anything here."

Only later did Thomas discover that there was an alcoholic Braidwood nephew, John, who'd tried and failed to extend the monopoly in America. The family was not inclined to help any non-relative from Hartford, Connecticut. Thomas continued to make appointments with Dr. Watson and Mr. Townshend, with members of the committee and of a subcommittee. He sent reports home to Hartford by ship and hunted for material on deaf-mutes in every bookshop of London. He read in one shop of the oral pioneer in eighteenth-century Germany, the tyrannical Samuel Heinicke, who wouldn't divulge his methods "except for money," and he uncovered a rare seventeenth-century treatise on deafness by the Scotsman George Dalgarno. After hours of reviewing books, Thomas' suppers were often spent with friends of the governor of Connecticut. He had looked up a minister he'd met at Yale, Robert Hall, who asked him to preach on Sundays in a small church.

Now in the conference room, Thomas gazed through the asylum window at the church spires rising above the tableau of brick and stucco buildings. Fog was wreathing the soot-tipped chimneys. The committee had been counting seventy-three tickets for review. On the hall stairs, frightened children clung together, a bleak sea of tattered clothing, and then an imperious Dr. Watson strode across the floor to call out to a guard the names of those subsidized to a Braidwood education. The list, Thomas noted, was painfully short. Sixteen names were pronounced. Sixteen silent waifs, out of a total of seventy-three.

The chosen ones were tapped on the head by the guard at the stairs. Shuddering, his vision slightly blurred, Thomas followed the rejected ones as they sadly filed down to the bottom floor. There Dr. Watson's hand clamped his shoulder. Would he care, the principal asked, to observe some of the students learning the trade of cutting leather?

Thomas agreed, knowing he was being thrown only a crumb, and in the unheated leather goods room he watched disheveled young girls and boys punching holes into leather straps. The scene duplicated pictures Thomas had viewed of the dingy workhouses where hapless street urchins labored day and night for a few meager shillings.

On a stained wall of the leather goods room hung a framed motto in Latin and English words:

Vox oculis subjecta
Voice Made Subject to the Eyes

The deaf, Thomas knew, would need to depend on their sight, but what of their hands? When he'd mentioned sign language and the manual alphabet to Dr. Watson, the principal had stormed into a fury. Sign, Dr. Watson said, was a dirty, sloppy, and vile activity totally forbidden at the Kent Road "oral" asylum. Decent deaf people did not use sign. They tried to lip-read and speak. Any children caught signing were deprived of a day's meals, and the hands of repeated offenders were tied with rope for a week.

Thomas leaned over a wooden bench, envisioning the winged images of sign gliding in splendid flight. The Braidwoods' rejection of signing seemed based on the fear of losing power over their students, of having the deaf set free. On a workbench, Thomas glimpsed a strange silver instrument, flattened on one side and on the other raised into a marble-shaped ball. Inquiringly, he looked at the nearest student, a thin boy of about twelve who was stitching a pair of shoes.

The boy checked to his left and right, as if to determine his safety, then took a broken slate and piece of chalk from

36

his lap and scribbled four sentences. "To teach speak," the boy wrote of the silver instrument. "To bend tongue in place. Much hurt. Don't like speak."

Thomas stepped closer, overjoyed at the chance to communicate with a student. The boy's bony hands scrubbed at the written words and offered the slate to him. "Ta-a-lk?" the boy said aloud in a blurred and thickened sound.

Thomas picked up the chalk to write a return question— any question. What had the boy learned? Did he have more words than Alice Cogswell? Did he ever use sign? Had his hands been tied with rope? But the door swung open and Dr. Watson was hovering over the workbench. Scowling at the student, the principal retrieved the outstretched slate. Time to leave, Thomas was told. If the American minister were so set on acquiring oral methods, he'd have to consider a bonded contract to the asylum. Was he interested? The contract would indenture him to live at Kent Road for a period of three to five years. He'd be expected to work eleven hours a day with no recess for midday meal. He would be assigned to penmanship class until Dr. Watson and the committee gave him permission to move onward.

In his diary, Thomas described the contract as "too monstrous a sacrifice of time and patience." Angrily, he penned a note of refusal to Dr. Watson. The Braidwoods doled out what they knew he must refuse. He couldn't spend three or more years in England. He had left America to acquire, in approximately one year, some oral teaching skills and further instruction in sign. Hopefully, he would become principal of a new school. "Shall I be treated," he wrote home to Dr. Mason Cogswell, "like a mere apprentice whom his master must chain lest he make his escape?"

A week later, Thomas walked from under the fog-

37

swathed awning of his hotel toward an address printed on a slip of paper. A bookshop clerk had told him that, in spite of the Braidwood opposition, a sign language demonstration was scheduled in London by the very Abbé Sicard of Paris whose books Thomas had used to teach Alice Cogswell. Hurrying alongside a street edged with plum trees, he flexed his fingers at the prospect of using the hand gestures and letters he'd put aside in Europe. Was he homesick for sign? he asked himself. Well, he supposed he was.

At a curb, the fog wrapping around him, he waited for the street to clear of carriages, but suddenly his chest constricted and he felt a heaviness that ached through his throat. His old breathlessness was overwhelming him. Yet he'd been feeling so well, and he had no time for illness. He must attend the Abbé Sicard's demonstration.

Supporting himself against a lamppost, Thomas opened his mouth to the fog. A street peddler grinned at him and spit into a porticoed doorway. Slowly, Thomas sucked in a breath. He inhaled and exhaled gradually, as if he were keeping rhythm with the roll of the fog—inching precious air into his lungs.

Finally, he could thrust himself from the post, brushing the sleeve of the peddler's coat and continuing on toward the address written down by the clerk. No matter how hard it was to breathe, he was determined to find the Abbé Sicard. The breathlessness, the aching, no longer were important to him. He would reach past pain—past the pain of his own struggle for air or the pain of the deaf-mutes who lived in exile—for some answers to take home to Hartford like a golden and glorious treasure chest of pearls.

From the Braidwoods, as Thomas had written to Dr. Cogswell, he'd gained nothing but demands for a "useless sacrifice of time." Perhaps the Abbé Sicard would be more willing to teach the silent method and might even invite Thomas to the institute in Paris. An American school for the deaf could function quite adequately with the natural language of sign. Oral methods could someday be added. Yet when they were, Thomas assured himself, they would be added with grace. There must be no outlawing of sign or no cruelty with a strange silver instrument that hurt the mouth or tongue. There must never be cause for any deaf child to hold up his broken slate and scribble the words, "Don't like speak."

The astounding exhibition at London's Argyle Room was attended by the Bishop of London and the Duchess of Wellington. Thomas watched in awe as the thin, white-haired Abbé Sicard led his educated deaf-mute assistants, Jean Massieu and Laurent Clerc, through a flawless demonstration of sign. Laurent Clerc, a young man in his midtwenties, answered an audience question on education, translated for him into the hand gestures. "Education," wrote Clerc in English on a blackboard, "is the care taken to cultivate the mind of youth, to elevate their hearts, and to give them the knowledge of the sciences and of that which is necessary to teach them to conduct well in the world."

After the meeting, Thomas wove through the animated crowd to introduce himself to the Abbé and was indeed invited to the Paris institute. "He promised me every facility," Thomas wrote Mason Cogswell, "to proceed regularly through the classes in their order 'til I make myself master of the whole system."

Sailing from London, and intending a short stop at the

one oral asylum in Edinburgh, Scotland, before arriving in France, Thomas was accused by the English newspapers of "sinful intrusion" upon the sacredness of promissory bonds. The Braidwoods fed on public trust and had convinced several publishers of the daily presses to defend the family's iron fortress of secrets.

In Edinburgh, four hundred miles up the coast from London, Thomas met the headmaster of Scotland's Institute for the Deaf and Dumb. He was dismayed to find that Mr. Kinniburgh was bound to the Braidwoods by a seven-year contract. Only Paris held out any promise, but the Scots at the inn where Thomas lodged warned of the chaos in France that had followed the Emperor Napoleon's fall, and persuaded him to postpone his journey.

From August, 1815, until March, 1816, Thomas lived in the city of Edinburgh. Though he had letters of introduction, and was asked to preach at a small chapel, he knew few people and once more spent his time roaming through the bookshops. His father wrote that the family was moving to the marketing center of New York City, but he received no other mail in Scotland and was increasingly lonely. His funds were vanishing and at last, in early March, he left for France, in the steerage of the ship *Buecleuch*. Safely disembarked in Paris, he followed directions from a uniformed gendarme to a small hotel near the river Seine, and the next morning he was welcomed at the Royal Institution for the Deaf and Dumb by the smiling Abbé Sicard. France and the United States, said the Abbé, would be united in rescuing the deaf. In two or three months, Thomas would learn everything of sign. He would see how expertly the students performed at reading, writing, and using the godly gift of their own hand language.

Jean Massieu and Laurent Clerc lived at the Royal Institution and were pleased that Thomas knew enough French from studies at Yale to converse with them on a slate. Laurent Clerc's class in communication was the most advanced at the school, and Thomas would stop in the classroom doorway just to enjoy the fluency of silent words. At night, he and Clerc, polishing each other's French and English, engaged in long hours of sign conversation. As a child, the deaf assistant had been taught to voice several sounds, but a tutor once hit him so roundly on the jaw for mispronouncing a word—causing him nearly to bite off his tongue—that Clerc had refused ever to speak aloud again.

From Laurent Clerc's fingers, Thomas learned the story of the remarkable Abbé Charles Michel de l'Épeé, a priest in a tiny eighteenth-century French hamlet who'd happened upon two deaf daughters of a parish family. The daughters could cook and sew, yet like all the neglected deaf of France, they understood little. The Abbé had taken them under his care. With an old Spanish textbook of manual letters, he taught the girls to read, write, and communicate, and soon he was teaching other deaf students. His classes eventually became the Royal Institution in Paris and drew attention to his silent method. The Abbé Sicard asked to be his assistant, and before l'Épeé's death the two priests worked to feed, clothe, and educate their deaf charges, virtually starving themselves to do so.

Oral training, said Laurent Clerc, had been an experiment at the institute, bits of the method having been smuggled out of England and Germany. Thomas was finally able to learn that oral sounds were taught by having a deaf pupil lip-read and place fingertips on the speaker's throat so that sound vibrations could be felt and gradually reproduced.

Mirrors were held in front of teacher and pupil to show tongue and mouth positions. But, explained Clerc, lipreading was made difficult by the visual similarity of many letters. Not even a third of spoken conversation made sense to a deaf lip-reader, and vocalized speech from a deaf-mute might sound confusingly thick and toneless. To the Abbé Sicard and his students, the oral method had seemed unnatural.

The quick, expressive flow of sign, Laurent Clerc spelled out to Thomas, was the key to unfettering the deaf from muteness. With hand gestures, deaf people—even tiny children—could speak among themselves and to others. They weren't straining to imitate what they could not hear. Their arms, hands, and fingers, the expressiveness of their whole bodies, were the instruments for transporting feelings and ideas.

By early June, Thomas had become proficient in every aspect of training offered by the Institution. As a warm sun poured like butter onto the boulevards of Paris, he thought of the sunlight of home. "Indeed," he wrote in his diary, "I long to return." Signing was now automatic to him, and he noticed that even during conversation with a hearing person his hands would move instinctively toward the gestures of his other language. His health, except for a few attacks of the breathlessness, had not taxed him, and at the Paris Chapel of the Oratoire he'd preached fifteen sermons to an English-speaking congregation.

If any worries over his health still tempered Thomas' thoughts about becoming principal of an American school for the deaf, his fears were allayed by Laurent Clerc's proposal to accompany him home to Hartford and help establish the school. The Abbé Sicard gave his blessings, and in an emotional finale a letter arrived unexpectedly from Alice Cogswell.

Thomas tore open the small envelope. On a lined piece of paper, the child who once stared so blankly at the letters *H A T* in the sand had composed a message of over two hundred words. Alice wrote of school lessons taken in her home:

"This morning study all in school away Geography all beautiful all very beautiful. . . . O come back little while— O all very glad—O beautiful—I love you very much—Your affectionate Alice Cogswell."

Eyes glistening, Thomas wiped his glasses and tucked the letter into his pocket. That same afternoon, he skipped classes at the institute to book passage on the ship *Mary Augusta.* He was ready to close the door on his fourteen-month-long European journey. *I'm coming home,* he mouthed silently to Alice Cogswell. It seemed to him, he wrote later, that on some level past sound, the child would be able to *hear* him. But just to be sure, he'd made a tapping gesture at his mouth and lower cheek with the closed finger-tips and thumb-tip of his right hand, lingering with relief and joy over the sign word for "home."

Chapter
Five

Images of cities revolved like pictures on a toy top—store-lined streets, tile-roofed meeting halls, hotel rooms bedecked with quilted bed coverings and flowered washbowls. Having docked in New York harbor on August 9, 1816, Thomas and Laurent Clerc had gone fund raising: in New York City, where Thomas preached and was reunited with his family on John Street, in Hartford, Boston, New Haven, Albany, Burlington, Salem, and Philadelphia. Once, rotten eggs were hurled onto a bandstand and the two men called tricksters, but the next city on their route was more hospitable.

Between trips, Thomas and Clerc rested in Hartford, staying at the Cogswells' and exchanging French and English. Their fingers, unwinding tales of their travels, would fly at Alice and at Dr. Cogswell, a serious student of sign, but soon—after pats on the back by the doctor and repeated hugs from his daughter—the wayfarers would be off again, trunks piled at the Jeremy Addams for the coach that left before dawn.

In the various meeting halls, Laurent Clerc was asked to exhibit his ability to reason, and to read, write, and sign. Approaching a podium, he was introduced by Thomas as the first school-educated deaf person on the streets of America. Curiosity seekers jammed the halls, flanked by the openly hostile and sneering, and Clerc could feel the vibrations of gasps as he showed audiences that an understanding of ideas did not depend on the hearing of words.

In Boston, Nathaniel F. Moore, the president of Columbia College, challenged Clerc to questions and answers at a three-legged easel. What were the opinions of the young Frenchman on Virtue? asked Moore. "It is," wrote Laurent Clerc to shocked applause, "the disposition or habit of the soul to do good, to avoid evil, and to observe what divine and human laws order and what reason dictates."

At the conclusion of the easel-writing, Thomas encouraged questions from the audience and translated them into sign for Clerc. Receiving the answers from his friend's hands, he spoke them aloud. Clerc sat down, then, by the easel and Thomas talked of what he'd learned in European books about the plight of the deaf. Throughout history, he said, grave errors in thinking had caused the nonhearing to live in anguish. Ever since A.D. 170, when Galen the physician assumed a common brain spot for speech and hearing, deafness had been linked to stupidity as well as muteness. Even the Roman Pliny the Elder had stated, "There are no persons born deaf who are not also dumb." But dumbness, Thomas explained, was not a necessary product of deafness.

The errors had multiplied, he said. Some people believed

deafness was a brain defect rather than an abnormality of the ears. Doctors were proving otherwise. Some called it a punishment by God for wrongdoing or for Original Sin. In Germany, in the 1700s, a Pastor Granau claimed that God wished the deaf to live in ignorant silence and that no one should tamper with their destiny by teaching them to understand. Yet, Thomas asked, hadn't Christ himself restored hearing and speech to a deaf-mute in an act of mercy and love? And didn't Leviticus, in the Old Testament, issue the command: "Thou shalt not curse the deaf"?

The Boston audience was becoming less wary, and Thomas told of several deaf-mutes who'd been gifted enough to overcome their silence. There were two deaf poets, the renowned Pierre de Ronsard and Joachim du Bellay, who had lived during the Renaissance in France. There was a sixteenth-century deaf artist, Juan Fernández Navarrete—*El Mudo*, "The Mute"—who became court-appointed painter to King Phillip II of Spain; and the German composer Ludwig van Beethoven, grown deaf as an adult, was the current rage of Vienna with his *Fidelio* and his Seventh Symphony. Yet for most of the deaf, Thomas said, life had been torment. Only education could give them language; and their hands were the tools of speech.

The winter months of 1817 slowed stagecoach travel to a virtual impasse, but Thomas and Laurent Clerc persuaded many a brandy-steeped coachman to rouse himself from a barroom, cork up his spirits bottle, and venture into the cold. The exhibitions in cities brought a growing number of pledges for a Hartford school for the deaf. Sufficient funds would mean that building space could be rented and supplies ordered. The ten merchants and educators of Hartford, joined by Mason Cogswell and presided over by a

46

Daniel Wadsworth, had incorporated themselves into a board of directors. The corporation won an unprecedented grant of $5,000 from the Connecticut legislature, the first appropriation of public money ever made in America for a charitable institution. More than $15,000, however, was necessary to cover expenses, and the board of directors kept prodding Thomas and Clerc, who'd traveled as much as they could, to visit every sizeable New England city.

By March, the total sum of mailed-in donations and pledges was tabulated at $17,000. Ecstatically, Thomas wrote to the Abbé Sicard in Paris that the brilliant Monsieur Laurent Clerc might one day melt the hearts of even hard-hearted Americans. Resistance continued, Thomas said, but with perserverance from the friends of the deaf it would weaken, and the mountains of doubt and scorn would slowly be chipped away.

Thomas began to hold meetings for parents and guardians of prospective students, rich and poor, for the Hartford school. Sometimes Alice rode along with him to the New Haven meetings, her blond hair braided into pigtails beneath her bonnet. To Alice, the idea of a school for deaf children was like imagining a fairyland. "Knowing without end," she kept signing to Thomas. "Knowing and knowing."

At one meeting, Thomas and Alice met a bearded farmer from nearby Guilford who drove them to his farm for supper and evening prayers. Miner Fowler introduced his guests to his wife and two deaf-mute daughters, Sophia and Parnell. The young women, age nineteen and twenty, had been deaf from birth—doctors did not know why—and used rough gestures to express their needs. They could do ordinary tasks, painstakingly taught them by father and mother, like spinning cotton or cleaning house, but otherwise they had existed for their parents as simple creatures of the farm, loved without reservation but not expected to achieve.

In the farmhouse, Sophia Fowler brushed her fingers over Alice's pigtails in wonderment, yanking impatiently at her own dark curls. With Mrs. Fowler's permission, Alice climbed on a stool to plait Sophia's hair into shiny braids. The older girl's cheeks blushed with pleasure as she watched her reflection in a brass kettle above the hearth. Transported by her new look, she smiled at Alice and Thomas, and when her father ushered everyone outside to the yard she pulled on a knitted shawl and danced at his heels.

Miner Fowler stood on a mound of hardened earth and spoke with thankfulness of the plans for a Hartford school. He held the household Bible to the forehead of each daughter, gesturing away to the gray-streaked sky and to Thomas and the horse and wagon. After the Bible was again touched to foreheads, it was Sophia who comprehended her father's message and who, tugging at her sister's sash, let out a gleeful, astonished yelp.

She guesses, Alice signed to Thomas, *at going someplace to learn. She guesses that you teach knowing and knowing.*

He nodded. Sophia guesses, Thomas acknowledged to himself, from the crude pantomime invented by her mother and father. Soon, she would not have to guess. She, and many others, could learn an official, structured language for hands and fingers. She could possess Solomon's "words of understanding"; with them might dream her own dreams of "what *might* be."

48

Parnell Fowler, quieter than her younger sister, waited by a rusted water pump, her eyes fixed on Alice's signs. But dark-haired Sophia began bouncing her red-checked skirt and white petticoats over her ankles and could not stay still. Dancing around a bare elm tree, her newly fashioned pigtails whipping behind her, Sophia kept smiling at Thomas and merrily tapping her forehead with the palms of her hands. The young woman, he saw, was as gay as if she were not burdened by silence.

At the time for leavetaking, a hearty supper had been served and prayers read in the candlelight. Thomas lifted a sleepy Alice into Miner Fowler's wagon for the return ride to New Haven. Harnessing his horse, the farmer stood at least six inches taller than the twenty-nine-year-old minister, but the expression on his face made it clear he looked up to Thomas, who proffered to Sophia and Parnell the kind of nourishment they could not find at home, however loving it was.

As the wagon rattled and swayed down the road away from the farm, Thomas took a notebook from his waistcoat pocket and carefully added the names of Sophia and Parnell Fowler to his list of students for the proposed school. Pebbles popped against the wheels and elms whispered as the night wind stirred their still leafless branches, but Thomas could only see the exuberant flurry of Sophia Fowler's tree dance. Next to the letters of her name, he impulsively added the four extra words, "A rare and radiant maiden."

Spring blossoms spread across the lawns and gardens of Hartford, confirming the end of winter in a panoply of color. On Prospect Street, not far from the Cogswell house,

49

the board of directors had rented a vacant building for the school, with space for both classrooms and dormitory facilities. Meals, said board chairman Daniel Wadsworth, would be taken by students and faculty across the street at the City Hotel.

Neither Thomas nor Laurent Clerc, who'd been approved as instructor by Mr. Wadsworth, were consulted in choosing the school quarters. With a dissenting vote from Mason Cogswell, the board had granted itself the power to make all administrative decisions. Thomas, of course, was elected principal, but the final say on policy matters and organization was to come from Daniel Wadsworth and the ten other members.

A faint warning had dampened the joy that propelled Thomas through the empty rooms of the Prospect building. The board's power reminded him of the Braidwood monopoly. How quickly good intentions could disappear. Yet writing in his diary, he described his work as beginning, and nothing could really diminish his pleasure at unpacking the books bought in London, Edinburgh, and Paris. A desk from the Cogswell attic was placed in the room selected for his office, and he covered its top with notepads and with boxes of clay and graphite pencils.

On a whitewashed wall, Thomas mounted a wide block of wood that had been carved with the manual alphabet by his brother Charles. All of the Gallaudets had sent their good wishes. Tracing Charles' raised letters with his finger, Thomas saw that even blind and deaf children like Julia Brace could follow the twenty-six shapes. He hoped to teach something of lipreading and oral speech, to improvise with whatever methods were useful. The new school would be a tribute to all who believed, as had the eighteenth-century French Academy of Sciences, that "the deaf could become capable of reasoning and acting like others."

On Tuesday, April 14, 1817, Thomas and Laurent Clerc finished painting the conference room for the board of directors. The following morning was scheduled for the formal opening of the school. Daniel Wadsworth and the board had voted and settled on a school name that disturbed Thomas—Connecticut Asylum for the Education and Instruction of Deaf and Dumb Persons—but for the moment he thrust aside his feelings about the words *asylum* and *dumb* and about the board's dictum that he teach six hours a day along with handling a full-time principal's duties.

Dropping his paintbrush into a jar of turpentine, needing to clear his chest of fumes, he strolled down Prospect Street with Laurent Clerc. At the Cogswell house, he left Clerc, telling him that he would return at supper. The walking appealed to him, though he had no special destination in mind. He felt an urge to retrace and recall. Walking on tree-lined Main Street, he passed the Hartford Bank, the pharmacy, the shoemaker's, the millinery shop. Three men at the barber's tipped their hats to him.

When he reached the Jeremy Addams, Thomas stood as he had on that chest-aching night in his sixteenth year. The tavern window was half-closed by a shade. The ruts in the dirt yardway could have been the same stagecoach tracks of that long-ago August night. Another loose carriage wheel leaned against the worn hitching post and Thomas bent toward it. Would he still be told to find an upping stone if he tried to lift the wheel?

Behind the tavern building, he set off across a meadow

where a hat factory was under construction, and he wandered down a labyrinth of roads to the old Wyllys estate. His black leather shoes sank slightly in the loam, which was softened by April rains, but he found the gnarled Charter Oak and the jagged hole in its bark. Yesterday merged into the present, and he could almost see his brother and friends racing off to the woolen mills, while he had lagged achingly in their trail.

Evening light was bathing the houses on Prospect Street when Thomas returned from his walk to the building that would witness the arrival, on Wednesday, of deaf-mute students. Climbing the steps, he unlatched the front door and pushed inward. A slanting beam of sunlight made the small vestibule glow, a tomorrow promise. Would he be equal to the unknown tomorrows that lay ahead? Lawyer, tutor, merchant, minister, he repeated to himself . . . and now, in spite of his frailties, principal of an American school for the deaf. He must preserve the joyfulness. He'd met someone in March who'd not lost the joy.

In the morning, Miss Sophia Fowler might dance across the school threshold, leading six other needy and uprooted young people from Thomas' list. Like the overture to a grand dance, he heard the melodious roll of their names: Alice Cogswell, Julia Brace, George Loring, Joseph Wenk, Parnell Fowler, Fisher Ames Spafford. . . .

Chapter
Six

The boy streaking down the banister had carrot-orange hair and a lopsided grin. Eleven-year-old Joseph Wenk's hearing loss only intensified the sharpness of his other four senses and his delight in testing them. Thomas could barely keep track of the child. Joseph was forever sliding, running, climbing, tasting. He peered into closets and drawers to juggle anything not bolted down. Since learning to speak in sign, his hands and arms were in perpetual motion.

Not all the children had adjusted so rapidly to the school. George Loring, the youngest pupil at age ten, wept for days from homesickness. Julia Brace was led into the classrooms by Laurent Clerc but kept screaming if anyone but Clerc tried to touch her. At the end of the second Wednesday, eight more children had arrived. One of the girls uttered loud braying noises whenever she was hungry. A pudgy, thirteen-year-old boy curled himself into a heap on a cot, refusing to uncurl. And permeating the rooms in those early weeks, before fear turned to confidence, was the odor of soiled clothing.

Most of the students of the asylum were, for the first time, separated from the familiarity of home. Mothers and fathers weren't available to decipher squeals, grunts, and whimpers. Strange scenes met the students and strange faces hovered over them; their fingers throbbed from being guided through the manual letters. Sometimes they clenched their hands against the signs.

Slowly, Thomas was able to calm the distress and confusion. Again and again, he signed the word for *tears* and the word for *smiles*—signing the words so persistently that, by the month's end, the discovery of a connection between the thing and its name had ignited a flame of excitement. Whatever it was in Thomas that had gained Alice Cogswell's trust was extended toward the other children. They could see his caring as something to rest on, to receive. They sensed how keenly this gray-eyed, clean-featured man struggled to teach them. If he was busy showing the school to visitors or sitting with the board of directors in the conference room, the students found refuge with the girl who danced so merrily through the halls. The pen-mark *S,* they were being taught, began her name-word.

Classes were organized in alphabet, writing, reading, and sign. Hand exercises were given to strengthen the muscles of fingers. Later on, Thomas introduced courses in grammar, history, arithmetic, geography, speech, furniture building, shoemaking, and sewing. The teaching of a trade, especially one needing scant communication, might provide older students with a means of support. Thomas allowed even Julia Brace to experiment with sewing, and to his amazement the blind girl could thread a needle with tongue and teeth and sew dresses by touch. Julia's screaming, kicking, and swearing stopped. She traced her fingers over Thomas' to master the manual alphabet. In the girls' dormitory, she proved to a flabbergasted Laurent Clerc that she could smell stray pieces of clothing and return them, without error, to the cot of each owner.

Thomas watched his pupils' hands opening to sign and the alphabet like the beaks of baby birds. The moments of awareness seemed, each time, miraculous. But could he teach enough, he wondered in his diary, in the four years per pupil allotted by the legislature? "I yearn," he wrote of his students, "to be their instructor, their guide, their friend, their father. How much is yet to be done before this can be accomplished. . . . If success finally crowns my efforts, to Him be all the glory."

Success, however, did not always crown Thomas' efforts. The board of directors had no experience at supervising an entire school. While they crowed over letters hailing the asylum as the "birthday of organized philanthropic effort in America," they argued heatedly over salaries, hirings, and firings. Thomas caught a hired houseman shoving a student against a wall. He asked for the man's dismissal, but a majority of the board claimed that since all employees might have their difficulties, Thomas would simply have to tolerate the "minor outbursts of temper."

In midwinter, when ice hung from the dormers of the school and the enrollment had risen to twenty-seven students, sickness attacked the children. High fevers and convulsions raged in the dormitories, and the sign words for "Mommy" and "Daddy" were formed by a succession of trembling and pleading hands. Dr. Cogswell was away from Hartford and Thomas hurriedly summoned another doctor from town, but Dr. Leonard Byers couldn't identify the malady. Alcohol baths were prescribed, and the boiling of nightclothes and bed linen.

Thomas offered the doctor a cup of tea and a seat in his office. The danger to his students, he was told, was in the possibility of sickness spreading through already damaged ears into the brain. The ear, remarked the doctor, was vulnerable to infection. Common also were ear abnormalities at birth or accidental punctures, in a fall, of the *tympanum*, the eardrum. Some of the students had probably gone deaf from high fevers. Others might have suffered a locking of the three tiny bones in the middle ear cavity— the hammer, anvil, and stirrup—which would keep sound waves from being transmitted further.

The students, Thomas promised, would be carefully tended. He would see that the linen and nightclothes were boiled. Deafness required courage enough without the addition of illness.

Dr. Byers agreed. Medical research into hearing was still in its infancy, he said. Sound waves were thought to pass from the air down the ear canal into the eardrum. There, the waves set the three bones of the middle ear vibrating, carrying sound into the inner ear where it became electrical impulses registered in the brain. But what was the exact function of the shell-shaped cochlea in the inner ear? And how did differently shaped sound waves—rough, smooth, long, short—affect timbre and pitch? Deafness was thought to occur from the ear's mechanical failure to transmit sound or from incurable damage to nerve cells or fibers, yet new research would build on the work of major theorists like Perrault, Kircher, Schellhammer, Cotugno.

At the end of nine days of torturing fevers, the unnamed

illness abated. The children were pale and weak, but their sickness hadn't invaded ear cavities or brain. Thomas had slept so seldom and climbed the stairs so often that his legs buckled under him. His eyesight had worsened, his chest was aching, and his throat was raw. One weekend in February, he found a note from Daniel Wadsworth in the chilled vestibule. A third instructor had been hired for the growing asylum, a man whose tenure would begin on Monday. As to salary, said Wadsworth, the teacher would be paid more than Thomas, being a "secular person" and not a minister of God.

Folding the note in half, Thomas glimpsed his reflection in the vestibule glass. His eyes looked bloodshot; his complexion sallow. Sinking onto a horsehair sofa, he leaned against the cushions. His salary at the school was small, and several board members—including Mason Cogswell—had tried to raise it. But eight of the members outvoted the other three. Since Thomas hadn't pressed for additional money, the board was content to underpay him.

He had written in his diary, "Teach me more self-denial and humility," but he realized the board was taking advantage of him and that he might not make a good case, even to himself, of his turning the other cheek. He'd felt an "undue anxiety," however, a "shrinking from difficulties" over discussing his salary, over seeing properly to "his own personal, temporal concerns."

A soft hand touched his shoulder. Startled, Thomas sat up, his gaze captured as it had been on the farm in Guilford by the radiance of Sophia Fowler. The young woman had recovered quickly from the sickness. At rows of other bedsides, she'd fed hot broth to the feverish, and when George Loring was convulsed with seizures she'd cradled the child in her arms. Gently now, Sophia lifted her right hand from Thomas' shoulder to touch her fingertips to her forehead, then to tap her stomach with the other hand. *Sick?* she had signed.

Thomas shook his head. How good it was to him that the sign had slipped so easily from Sophia's hands, that he and she could talk together. *Not sick,* he signed back, then put the fingertips of both his hands at the sides of his waist and drooped them slightly. *Tired, Sophia,* he signed, spelling out her name. *Only tired.*

The young woman seemed satisfied that her teacher was in no peril. She curtsied, smiled, and left the vestibule. Some moments later, feeling less drained, Thomas rose from the sofa and went down the hall to his office. His eyes had stopped stinging, but his hands tensed with a sudden impulse toward words. On the wall was his next day's schedule: six classes plus a tour of the school with a Pennsylvania state official; a conference with a New York philanthropist; letters of inquiry to be answered; a promised game of catch with Alice Cogswell and Joseph Wenk. He had best get a good night's sleep, but he sat unmoving at his desk. An indescribable longing gnawed at him, something he couldn't explain. He questioned whether he should allow any interference with his concentration on work, whether a "rare and radiant maiden" should bring such a lift in his mood.

Silence reigned in the office and in the corridors and classrooms, and Thomas was not yet ready with answers for the questions he'd asked.

At the center of Prospect Street, a platform had been constructed, its base draped with red, white, and blue skirting. Flags with fifteen stripes and fifteen stars billowed from poles and windows. The townspeople of Hartford, outfitted in their finery, had congregated to greet the carriage of the fifth president of the United States, the recently elected James Monroe. The president would appear on this May afternoon in 1818 to bestow sanction on the eight-month-old Connecticut Asylum and to commend its pioneering principal, the Reverend Thomas Gallaudet.

Politics blended with pride in the celebrations of the crowd. In the state election, the Democrats had badly defeated the Federalists, and a state constitution had been adopted that was to remain in force until the mid-1960s. The deaf students of the asylum—thirty-three in number—were seated on the platform, shirts and smocks pinned with patriotic ribbons. As the presidential carriage arrived, the children rose to salute, and Thomas and Laurent Clerc rushed into the street to escort President Monroe through the cheers and applause.

The president stood on the dais to thank his well-wishers and to speak of the asylum. Its founding, he said, was an oasis of humanity amid the world's deserts. All resources of the United States Government would be committed to bettering the fate of the nation's handicapped. That fate, said President Monroe, had been forever brightened on the day that a young man named Thomas Hopkins Gallaudet taught several words to a deaf-mute neighbor, Alice Cogswell. Now, Government legislators from each of the fifteen states were encouraging public education for the disabled.

The president's address was met by a full five minutes of applause. Afterwards, a sign language demonstration was performed by Thomas, Alice, and six of the students. Cheers shook the wooden supports of the platform, bringing smiles to the pupils. Sign, Thomas explained through a horn, was not only a natural device for the deaf. In the second to fourth centuries, signing had been practiced by actors of the Roman *pantomimi*. Actually, hand gestures and the manual alphabet were used by Cistercians and other monks. Everyone, said Thomas, formed some sort of individual or even universal "signs" when they gestured for emphasis, pointed to themselves, or beckoned a guest into a house. Organized and developed speech with the hands was proving as valid a language as communicating aloud with the mouth.

That afternoon, the children of the asylum created a new sign, one that would mean *president*. A pantomime was made of President Monroe's tricorn hat, both hands being placed half-open at the forehead, then snapping closed while drawing outward into a V-shape. The president had seemed flattered that his visit to Hartford prompted one of the first American sign words.

The celebration on Prospect Street focused worldwide attention on Thomas' work with the deaf. Mail covered the vestibule table, and the more replies Thomas wrote, the higher rose the pile. Still shaky from the days of illness at the school, he asked the board, which seemed increasingly domineering, to assign some correspondence to Laurent Clerc. His request was denied. The headmaster of the asylum, said Daniel Wadsworth, must be its spokesman. Besides, weren't Thomas' duties clearly defined? Surely he was conversant with them—teaching six daily classes, receiving visitors and scheduling tours, answering all correspondence, requisitioning domestic supplies, training new instructors, and conducting student exhibitions in cities to gain public and legislative backing? Sufficient work, Laurent Clerc remarked drily to Thomas, to wilt the strength of eleven men.

Thomas admitted that he knew he should insist on a reduction of duties, yet Dr. Cogswell had privately offered to help him with the mail—and besides, the school was nearing its summer vacation and his students were happy at writing words. Their silence had sprung alive with the "noise" of discovery, and he didn't want to disrupt it by teaching fewer classes or not traveling on the exhibitions. In the fall, Thomas said, he would try to confer with the board. In the fall, when the school was firmly established and harbored no sickness.

On June 10, Thomas helped the students pack up their clothes and class papers. Two days later, he was greeting the parents who arrived on the front steps. The sun warmed his face, but there was a deeper warmth in the embraces and farewells from his pupils. Fingers were spelling *September, September!* as hands signed *Thank you!* and *I'll miss you!*, and he realized that, indeed, he'd already begun missing the children. How would the banister squeak without Joseph to slide on it? How would the dormitory hooks fill with mended pinafores and knickers without Julia Brace? At least Alice and her parents would not be far away. At least Laurent Clerc was staying on in Hartford and, of course, there would be calls from neighboring parishes for preaching.

Miner Fowler came that day from Guilford, one of the last parents to mount the steps. The farmer, beard flecked with white, had brought early vegetables for Thomas and a jubilant hug for the two young women who waited at the door. Parnell Fowler, shy but serene, wore a slim gray dress, a quiet contrast to her sister's full-skirted yellow gown. Sophia's dark curls glistened in the sun. *It's summer,* she signed to Thomas. *I write you. Letter. You answer?*

Yes! Thomas nodded emphatically in return, a sudden lump constricting his throat. *I will answer,* he signed. *I promise. Happy summer, Sophia.*

Sophia smiled, nodded back, and ran from the steps toward her father's wagon. Two trunks were stacked in the wagon bed. As the sisters climbed on the front seat, waving at Thomas, Miner Fowler picked up the reins. Lumbering from side to side, the old mare dragged the wagon around a corner, and then Thomas was alone on the steps, staring into the vacant street. The sun had begun setting before a tug on his arm wrested him from his thoughts, and he glanced down at ten-year-old George Loring, the child who'd lain so feverishly in Sophia Fowler's arms during the sick time.

Timidly, the deaf boy presented a scrap of paper to his teacher and principal. On the top was a message penciled in his newly learned language. "School ends," George Loring had written. "Till September. I love very much Miss Sophia Fowler."

Thomas drew the child against him. The lump that filled his throat was growing larger and more painful. *Yes,* he reached to finger-spell into the sun-drenched air, finding a space where George Loring could see the letters. *Y-e-s,* he spelled again, more slowly and distinctly, his fingers throbbing like a heartache over the solitary word.

Chapter
Seven

The letter promised to Sophia—and others un-promised—were sent to Guilford over the summer of 1818. By August, Thomas had abandoned writing "My esteemed pupil" or "My dear pupil" for "My dear Sophia." But he couldn't bring himself to expose more of his feelings; he wrote of buying new books and pictures for the school, of a boat trip taken to New York to visit his family. Not for years did he learn that Sophia secretly tied all his letters together with a pink satin ribbon in order to save them "forever and always."

The fall semester at the school, and the three succeeding ones, found the enrollment at 125 students. In 1819, the school name was broadened in scope to the American Asylum, at Hartford, for the Education and Instruction of the Deaf and Dumb. Five associate instructors were hired and trained by Thomas in manual speech, and following Thomas' example, four experimental schools for the deaf opened in New York, Pennsylvania, Kentucky, and Ohio.

Many Americans still ridiculed the "wasted teaching of dummies"—and newspapers reported the case of a deaf-mute orphan being mutilated in the streets—yet the wasteland of deaf education was sprouting small, fertile pockets of learning.

In his classes, Thomas counted a word learned when it could be signed, if a sign existed, finger-spelled, written, and read. Facial expressions and body movements helped carry the emotion of a word or phrase. A widening of Thomas' eyes might convey astonishment; the forward motion of his head and torso could deliver a sense of curiosity. By communicating through gestures, or writing on a blackboard, or pointing to Charles' carved wooden letters, he filled the blankness with facts and ideas. History, geography, religion, and folklore entered the students' minds. Referring to ancient events, Thomas used the sign for *past* —a hand waving backwards over the shoulder. To indicate the future, he waved an open palm forward.

One of the newest students at the American Asylum appeared without introduction. Eighteen-year-old Tom Brown, a deaf-born farm boy, had traveled on horseback from New Hampshire to Hartford. Hammering his knuckles on the doorjamb, he'd indicated his interest in carpentry; scratching a finger across his shirt, he let Thomas know that he wanted to write.

Tom Brown was accepted as a student and worked diligently with his teachers. Once he'd mastered signs for *why* and *how,* he never stopped asking questions. If Laurent Clerc taught the sign word for *pen,* Tom demanded to be told the merits of *pen* over *pencil,* of how to make one himself. Supplied with goose and crow quills, he learned to boil them in alum for hardening and to sharpen the points with a knife until he had usable tools.

Three months after his arrival, Tom Brown was making fine-line and thick-line pens for Thomas' ledgers and impressing visiting townspeople with cabinet building and wood inlay. He learned to read, his big-knuckled right thumb pressing at each word on a page, and became so proficient that by his second year at the school he was poring over farm journals in Hartford's pharmacy. In his final semester, Tom was called home to nurse his elderly parents. He named the four sections of the family farm—orchard, pasture, woodland, and sugar bush—for Thomas and three other teachers.

In 1820, a much-publicized act of Congress granted a township of uncultivated land to the asylum. The sale of the land enabled the board to purchase property a half-mile from the center of Hartford, and construction began on a three-story frame building, facing south, that would eventually house the American Asylum under its third and most suitable name—the American School for the Deaf.

Dedication services were held at the completed school building on May 22, 1821. Thomas escorted guests through the classrooms, library, and workshops, preaching an afternoon sermon from the top of the outside stairs. "For we know," he quoted from Paul's second letter to the Corinthians, "that if our earthly house of this tabernacle were dissolved, we have a building of God, a house not made with hands, eternal in the heavens."

May had been blooming across the countryside, town, and school. Thomas, too, was filled with the stirrings of spring. Along one border of the school lot, he cultivated the soil for a flower garden, uprooting a buried landmarker etched with the name Scarborough—the former owner of the seven-acre plot. Restlessness sent him down Gurney's Road to the state house on a search for the Scarborough family roots, a project that distracted him from thinking of Sophia Fowler. Wasn't he her principal, he berated himself, a man who should keep his distance? Hadn't he avoided scheduling her in his classes? But in June, his restlessness turned to daring and he no longer fought his urge to look for Sophia to round the corner of every hallway.

Could he really dream of "what *might* be?" Aside from responsibility to his position, he was, Thomas wrote in his diary, eleven years Sophia's senior. And if that weren't sufficient, his frail health hardly made him a bargain for a young and beautiful woman. Yet hadn't he been of help to her? Didn't he, last semester, bring her boxes of reading books? Mightn't he become her permanent tutor and teach her of politics or law? Was there any hope that she could return his feelings?

On an evening when moths were beating their wings against the windows of the American School, Thomas drafted a proposal of marriage to Miss Sophia Fowler. Laboring over his words, he twice tore up the paper and started afresh. None of his debates, sermons, speeches, or articles had prepared him for persuading Sophia to be his wife. When he sealed the envelope with wax, leaving it on her pillow the next morning, he fled the dormitory room as if he'd just perpetrated some dastardly deed.

Sophia was overwhelmed that Thomas wished to marry her. If he considered his inadequacies, she had added up her own and found them too numerous to bear. She was

66

not, she reminded him, a "normal"; she was a never-hearing. She was twenty-three years old in the silence and only four years of age at naming the world's names. Even if she and Thomas could braid their lives, as Alice Cogswell had braided hair, what if she bore him a deaf child—tainted that child with her own blemish?

Not once, through all the years since he'd studied at Yale, had Thomas yearned so desperately to win a debate. His arguments had been presented to Sophia, and her counterargument was received. The chance for rebuttal was his. In a meeting in the school garden, Sophia stood beneath a walnut tree, and Thomas' hands were so filled with words they shot out before him like pistons. He talked of the "light" Sophia gave him, of how that light was more important than what he still could teach her. He talked of their being able to solve any problems together.

Love was the victor in the garden debate. On August 29, 1821, Thomas and Sophia were married in Center Church at Hartford. Parents, brothers and sisters, Laurent Clerc, and sixteen-year-old Alice Cogswell and her family attended the ceremony. The couple honeymooned in New York's Saratoga Springs, drinking the famed waters and climbing the foothills of the Adirondacks. While several guests at the Union Hall stared rudely at Sophia when she didn't acknowledge their greetings, resentment turned to pity when she was seen signing to Thomas. Yet Sophia Fowler Gallaudet needed no one's pity. Joy and vitality resided within her; she was, as Thomas had seen, imbued, if not with sound, with a splendid and radiant light.

Thomas and his bride moved into a tiny rented house within a mile of the school. The number 30 marked their door and Sophia, who'd brought her loom from Guilford, wove a doormat of hemp. The kitchen overlooked sycamore trees on the rear lawn and there Sophia rejoiced in the meals she cooked for Thomas. Laurent Clerc, who'd married a young hearing woman named Elizabeth Boardman in the spring of 1819, was on a seven-months leave of absence to help organize a school for the deaf in Pennsylvania, but other teachers and students were invited to suppers.

The talk over the table was conducted in sign, and Thomas would beam at the sophistication shown by Sophia. She was quickly able to understand a joke or a subtle change of meaning. She'd learned that in the growing vocabulary of American sign, the sign noun for *food* could indicate the verb *to eat.* The sign for *college,* if it was made upside down, referred to someone conceited about book learning.

Before bedtime, Sophia would sew or study vocabulary, and Thomas would work on articles he was writing for journals, newspapers, and magazines. His topics were often unpopular issues; he favored female education and the training of women as missionaries; he spoke out against slavery. A favorite topic was the need for the formal teaching of teachers. As it was, a novice teacher might be trained haphazardly by only one seasoned instructor. "We spend our labor," Thomas wrote, "upon the old trees; we too much disregard the young shoots."

For the American School, Thomas prepared an elementary book, a vocabulary book, and large-lettered word charts that he hung in the classrooms. Charts had never been used in the European schools for the deaf, but they became a staple—along with slates, pencils, paper, and Tom Brown's quill pens—in Thomas' classes. Traveling with his advanced pupils to exhibitions in New England, he watched the flowing hand sentences impress spectators anew and prompt state officials to apportion money for deaf education.

Success kept up its patchwork pattern at the American School. Thomas was more convinced than ever that all types of communication encouraged the deaf, and he added verbal speech and lipreading to his classes. The board of directors promptly voted to remove the oral methods. Whether truly opposed to oral training or trying to control Thomas and all curriculum changes, the board issued a report condemning verbal speech among the deaf as distorted "parlor tricks" that ranked students "little higher than starlings or parrots."

Thomas appeared at a monthly meeting to argue that oral methods allowed the hearing public to understand the deaf. While only a small percentage of deaf-born children could develop intelligible speech, those few might be less ostracized by society; and those deafened later in childhood, with some memory of sound, might be taught to imitate talking satisfactorily.

Nonsense, most of the board replied. Rather than listen to a jumble of words, the hearing would prefer to learn American Sign Language or to leave the deaf to themselves.

Thomas' troubles with the board of directors were intensifying. If he asserted what he believed, he was called "impertinent" or "intrusive"—though he'd never been ill-mannered when giving his point of view. And if he retreated from the conflict, he was pestered to attend meetings. He asked Mason Cogswell's advice, but the good doctor could only tell him to try and endure his trials with the more unreasonable board members. Then, in the spring of 1823, Thomas faced a crisis with a board-hired superintendent who was so jealous of him that he insisted on being called "the other head of the institution." The man diverted visitors from Thomas' office and intercepted the mail. Requisitions disappeared, and students were delayed in the corridors, arriving late to Mr. Gallaudet's classes. The board ignored Thomas' requests for a hearing, just as they'd once refused to fire the houseman who'd pushed a student into a wall. A hunger for control consumed the majority of the board members as totally as it had the Braidwoods.

The battle continued all summer. By the second week of fall semester, turmoil and friction at the school had spread like the first year's sickness. The students were depressed, and the five associate teachers were short-tempered and surly. On September 16, Daniel Wadsworth conceded that because of "demand and necessity," the superintendent would be discharged. But in a sudden lashing out at the very foundation of the school, one board member presented a motion for Thomas' resignation.

On September 17 and 18, the American School was a battleground. To escape the uproar of informed townspeople and faculty, the board planned a clandestine meeting at Morgan's Hotel in Hartford. Word of the meeting crept out, however, and the school's five associate teachers rented an adjoining room. They composed a "blackmail" letter, announcing in fury to the board that if the motion for Thomas' resignation were passed, the entire staff would resign.

Thomas stayed sequestered in his school office. He knew he was backing off from the conflict—and this time he couldn't excuse his behavior by writing of "humility" or "self-denial." Instead, he hoped for a greater adequacy at defending his own rights, not just the rights of the deaf. In his diary, he recorded his prayers to God: "I invite His grace to qualify me."

Wanting to spare Sophia the anxious wait in the office, Thomas hadn't explained to her the motion for resignation. But alone at his desk, he found that he needed his wife's cheerful optimism. When she came with supper in a basket, his eyes fixed upon her incandescent face. He remembered the class valedictorian vote at Yale that had gone to Gardiner Spring, but for a moment he couldn't remember if he must form his words for Sophia in sound or sign. Somehow, she listened to his deepest thoughts and feelings. Letting the words break, at last, through his fingers, he began telling her in detail of the meetings underway at Morgan's Hotel.

Sophia's gaze never wavered. *School is here because of you,* she signed. *God will see to the board.*

As the night wore on, Thomas became less sure that he should have vented his complaints about the superintendent. Yet how could he have functioned under such a regime? The cost, both to the school and himself, would have been immeasurable. His signs blurred, and then he felt Sophia's index finger touch his forehead, watched it crook and uncrook as she drew it away. *Dream,* she was signing. *Dream your dreams of what might be. . . .*

His cheek grazed the palm of her hand. *Forever and always,* he signed back.

Shortly past nine o'clock, a rowdy knocking began at the front door of the school. Thomas sped from his office and Sophia, having sensed the strong vibrations, was close be-

71

hind. Unlatching the door, Thomas saw the dark figures of the five associate instructors. One of them, Lewis Weld, grabbed his hands. "Victory!" the teacher shouted. "The board capitulated. The motion for resignation was voted down. You're still our principal—as well you should be!"

Thomas felt something open inside him. *The motion had failed!* He could breathe more easily and a cloudy film peeled from his eyes. Asking Lewis Weld about the vote, he realized how wounded he'd been in the last days.

The five instructors surrounded him to offer congratulations, and over their beaming faces he signed the news to Sophia. Silhouettes of other figures were crossing into the road, and he heard the salutations to him and the burst of applause.

Lewis Weld grew more serious and told Thomas how the town had lent its support, shopkeepers corralling the board members on Main Street to acclaim him loudly. Hartford was inspired by Thomas, said Lewis Weld. Purpose gripped the community, and the people wanted Thomas to stay. The board, they predicted, would never dare such an outrage again.

Thomas glanced over his shoulder into the shadowed hall that led to his office. How often he'd come to the door of the school—to begin, to welcome, to await tomorrows. "We've all been privileged to hear the same song," he said to Lewis Weld. "It reaches us out of the silence." Taking Sophia's arm in his, he stood with her by his side. "All the children of silence," he said, "must be taught to sing their own song."

Chapter
Eight

 From the early to mid-1800s, while thousands of European deaf children foraged in alleyways, begging coins of strangers and being cheated by peddlers, the countries of Ireland, Denmark, Sweden, and Russia began preliminary education of the deaf. By the year 1840, though the dreary asylum system was yet in force, Denmark passed a law making school compulsory for the nonhearing child.

In England, in 1825, Thomas Braidwood was dead and a Swiss educator named Louis du Puget assumed his duties. Manually trained, du Puget abruptly introduced sign and finger-spelling to oral schools of England and Scotland. The influence of France's silent method had extended to the British Isles, and signing was no longer a terrible offense. The ropes used for hand-tying disappeared. After a rule of more than fifty years, the Braidwood dynasty came to an end.

Fierce controversy over the oral or silent system con-

73

tinued to rage, however, in countries that made an attempt to count and educate their deaf. Instead of combining techniques for the benefit of deaf pupils, the proponents of each system refused an alliance. Only politics consistently effected any change. The Napoleonic Wars had swept sign and the manual alphabet into "oral" Germany in the baggage trains of French armies. But after Napoleon's fall, German nationalism had reared up against anything French, and a handful of teachers—including a Herr Johann Graeser—revived the oral system instituted in 1778 under Germany's Samuel Heinicke.

Johann Baptist Graeser of Bavaria was the first to experiment with combined classes—later called "mainstreaming" —of the hearing and nonhearing. Graeser taught his deaf students to lip-read for one to two years, then incorporated them into regular hearing classes. Mainstreaming was practiced in public schools in various German states but, after the 1820s, was abandoned when the deaf couldn't yet keep pace with hearing pupils.

In the United States, the veto of oral methods at the American School influenced the four schools in other states. Some of Thomas' graduates were hired as instructors by the New York and Pennsylvania schools, building an almost total reliance on finger-spelling and sign. Oral classes were not to be offered at the American School until 1895, and in spite of them, the division between the oral and silent camps would critically widen.

On his own, Thomas taught oral speech, though he continued to regard sign as the "natural" and "superior" language of the deaf. The process of lipreading, he saw, involved much tiring guesswork for a deaf pupil. *P, b,* and *m* looked identical on the lips, and words such as *mad, mat, bat, bad,* and *pat* could rarely be distinguished. But if, at best, the deaf decoded only a third of lip speech—and even if returned responses were grossly limited and slow—oral skills did at least let deaf and hearing communicate with each other.

By 1829, Lewis Weld had left his instructor's post at the American School to become principal of the school in Pennsylvania. Beforehand, Thomas and Weld traveled to Washington, D.C., to hold an exhibition of sign before Congress. Excitedly, Laurent Clerc waved them off on the stagecoach, sending regards to the politicians met on his own travels for public education of the deaf. Clerc had never gone back to live in his native France. The Abbé Sicard had died in 1822, and Clerc chose to remain permanently in the United States, teaching at the American School for a total of forty-two years.

Thomas and Lewis Weld acknowledged to Congress the great debt owed the Abbés l'Épeé and Sicard for their "singularly beautiful and impressive" signs. They demonstrated, however, that American Sign Language—sometimes called ASL—was not merely a copy of France's silent system but was developing into an authentic hybrid. In the first year of the American School, makeshift signs from New England deaf children had enhanced the vocabulary pictures on Thomas' charts.

While in Washington, Thomas was invited to preach in the hall of the House of Representatives. His founding of American education for the deaf had gained him such respect in the capital city that John Quincy Adams, sixth president of the United States, wrote a full account of the

Reverend Mr. Thomas Gallaudet's sway over congressional grants.

At home, in the warmth of Number 30, Asylum Street, Hartford, Sophia Gallaudet had nearly forgotten her fears about motherhood. A healthy son, little Thomas, was born in 1822, followed by a second child, Sophia; the next four years brought Peter Wallace and Jane, named after Thomas' parents; and, in 1829, William Lewis. All five babies, soon after birth, had started and cried when Sophia dropped a hearth kettle beside the cradle. Running joyfully to Thomas, her skirts dancing anew over ruffled petticoats, she'd signed, *The baby hears! The baby is not deaf!*

Thomas remodeled part of the house for a hearing schoolroom, pacing his strength for the heavier hammering and sawing. A teacher was hired at a modest fee to instruct the two older children, and Thomas invited three hearing boys and girls from the neighborhood to attend classes. Once a week, he listened to recitations and entertained the children with a Bible story or verse. Sophia would sit in the rear of the room with Jane or William Lewis nestled in her lap, and sturdy Peter Wallace would stand to watch "bigger sister and brother." The children learned to speak fluent sign, each taught the hand gestures for *mama* almost as soon as they could mouth the word.

Thomas returned from Washington with traveling trunks battered by his many stagecoach rides. He was met at the Jeremy Addams by Laurent Clerc, and the two men walked the familiar route down Main Street. In the past year, Clerc had earned extra money from the American School for tutoring novice instructors. Thomas had never received any increase in salary when he'd served as tutor. Efforts to strip him of authority had not entirely halted, though this time it was Laurent Clerc who tackled the board in his name.

A lost cause, Thomas signed to his friend. The board wanted him gone and, in truth, he was still not comfortable over facing the conflict with them. He distracted Clerc from the subject, pointing out a wagon crammed with marble gravestones and statuary parked by the millinery shop. The sight of the stones, sent a deep chill through Thomas, though in his diary he often wrote calmly of "the mansions of eternal rest." But the chill didn't seem connected to his own physical problems; he was seized by a strange sense of portent for someone else—someone far away or near, he wasn't sure.

The following autumn brought news that Thomas' thirty-eight-year-old brother Charles had died of illness. In New York, reunited with some of his family, Thomas sadly delivered the eulogy, recollecting the days when young Charles had outraced and outlasted him on the Connecticut hills. The funeral was not the first for a member of the immediate family. Thomas' mother, Jane, had also died, and death had claimed three other brothers: Edgar, William Edgar, and Wallace. Packing up the New York household, Thomas' father took a job with the United States Treasury in Washington.

In the waning days of 1830, Thomas experienced another chilling loss. On the tenth of the month, he celebrated his forty-third birthday. Sophia had arranged a birthday party for him in the school dining hall, students, teachers, and family signing their good wishes to the accompaniment of Laurent Clerc's piano tunes. Four children's books, machine-printed and bound in Boston and Philadelphia, were

77

given to Thomas for his hearing classes at home. He passed them around the room, remarking that stories for children weren't seen nearly often enough on American printing presses.

That evening, after the family was home from the party, Thomas helped Sophia put the children to bed. The house had settled into nightly hibernation—comforters tucked under small chins, curtains drawn, candles snuffed—when the last-minute murmurs and sleepy kisses were interrupted by the arrival of one of the Cogswells' servants. Dr. Cogswell, said the terrified young man, had been confined five days with winter pneumonia. Tonight he had suffered a fever crisis and just now died in his daughter's arms. Could Mr. Gallaudet pay a call on Prospect Street?

Thomas threw on his coat, signed the sad story to Sophia, and plunged into the wintery night with the teary-eyed servant. The light of an oil lantern barely penetrated the gusts of snow, and Thomas and the servant huddled over against the wind. Trudging at last onto the front walk to the Cogswells', they clung to each other to keep from slipping into the knee-high snow banks.

All the way from Asylum Street to Prospect Street, Thomas grieved at the loss of his old friend and worried that twenty-five-year-old Alice wouldn't be able to cope with this final, untappable silence. She'd once had only her father to believe she could truly think. Now her father was dead, and who could say what renewed loneliness and isolation might set off in the daughter?

Oddly, Alice was showing unusual calm. She served tea to her mother and to several aunts and uncles, and she hugged Thomas and offered him a chair in the parlor. As he spoke to the family of Dr. Cogswell's death, his prayers

78

were said, simultaneously, in sign, and Alice's hands joined in. While he assured Mrs. Cogswell that he would make funeral arrangements, Thomas even heard Alice laugh as she skittered across a melted snow puddle on the foyer floor.

Walking home through the blustery snow, the oil lamp relit, Thomas kept telling himself that everything was under control on Prospect Street, that Alice had evidenced no alarming despair. Yet another chill, more profound than the one he'd felt on Main Street with Laurent Clerc, was coursing through him. He must warm himself, he thought. He must not pay such heed to shiverings.

At half-past eleven, he was readying himself for bed near a slumbering Sophia when, once more, a Cogswell servant called at the house. Thomas was given further upsetting news. Miss Alice, said the servant, had collapsed. She'd dropped onto the stairs by the parlor, and not a soul could stop her keening. Her hands were speaking *father* and also *teacher*. Teacher, whispered the servant, was how poor Miss Alice always talked of Mr. Gallaudet. Could he attempt a second visit on his own birthday night? Mrs. Cogswell, aware of the snow and cold, sent heartfelt appreciation.

Alice was wildly hysterical. Lurching out of her mother's arms, her blond hair askew, she ignored Thomas and pounded her head against the parlor hearth, scraping her fingers over the stones so they bled. White foam oozed from the corners of her mouth. Gently, Thomas restrained her, but she twisted away, curling fetuslike into her father's armchair. *I'm here,* Thomas spelled into her palm. *I'm with you. I'm here.*

The reassurance, spelled and respelled, scarcely penetrated Alice's delirium. Exhausted, she allowed herself to be carried into her bedroom. On the bed, an afghan folded around her, she lay staring into space. Waiting nearby, Thomas kept signing and spelling his affection and care.

Alice looked up at her beloved teacher. Her eyes filled with tears and haltingly she moved her hands from beneath the afghan. *Dead,* she signed, opening and closing her palms like a shell. *Father's dead. I die, too.*

No! Thomas signaled. He shook his head, confounded at how deceived he'd been earlier that evening by the young woman's calm. He saw her now as she'd looked to him sixteen years before, excluded from a boisterous circle of "normal" children, watching forlornly from her prison. Who, beyond her father and mother, had really known the suffering of her earliest years? And who, except father, had studied her deafness in books or preserved the hope of awakening the sleeping, afflicted beauty?

His hands jumping over themselves in haste, Thomas was signing a rash of words. He told Alice how much her father had wished her to live and prosper, how proud he'd been of her. *You and I,* he signed, *are settlers in the special land of knowing and knowing. The American School wouldn't have taught anyone without you.*

Alice smiled slightly. Tiptoeing into the parlor, and leaving Mrs. Cogswell to tend her daughter, Thomas picked up his top hat and brought it into the bedroom. Hooking the snow-dampened hat over one of the wooden bedposts, he smiled at Alice. *HAT,* he finger-spelled—then signed, *Do you remember?*

She nodded. With a faraway gaze, she seemed to retrieve momentarily that June day on the porch steps of Thomas' house. Her hands loose, almost limp, she signed *Thank you.* A tear rolled down her cheek, mixing gratitude with grief, and she read the question from his fingers: *Would she please try to sleep?* Her nod was subdued, obedient.

Thomas marked the shallow rhythm of her breathing. Each inhalation was ragged, reminding him of his own gasping spasms. He drew in some air as if he might breathe for her. Who, he wondered, could fill her fatherless void? *Teacher* was not sufficient. The four years at the American School were far behind her, and higher education—preparatory school or college—did not exist for the deaf. At least, it hadn't.

Alice's eyelids were fluttering and Thomas formed the sign for *Good night.* His right hand dipped down past his raised left hand and arm like the sun receding at the horizon. Briefly, Alice signed her reply, and Thomas turned with Mrs. Cogswell to leave the bedroom. He would not be making a third trip to the Cogswell house on this cold night, but he'd soon be called back. Perhaps he suspected as much when, home once more with Sophia, he replayed the goodnight between himself and Alice. He'd assumed, hadn't he, studying her across the room, that she'd signed *Good night* to his *Good night?* Yet he might have seen only what he wished to see.

In retrospect, as December 10 lapsed into the early hours of the eleventh day, Thomas was not at all certain of Alice Cogswell's reply. Her hand had lifted from the afghan, then inclined. Her eyes had trembled shut; a shadow, he recalled, fell over her. *Good night?* he puzzled in his diary. Not *good night.* In his mind's eye, he watched Alice elevate her hand. Her fingers moved toward him, bent inward.

With sudden trepidation, Thomas saw the actual word. Alice had not signed *Good night* to her cherished teacher. She had, instead, bid him *Good-bye.*

Chapter
Nine

Thirteen days after the death of her father, Alice followed him to the grave. She had stopped eating, as deafened to life as were her ears to sound. She was buried the morning before Christmas, earth relegating her coffin to infinite silence.

Hartford celebrated the year's end with dance assemblies in the public hall. Thomas did not join in the general merriment or the boastful resolutions made for January 1. For him, the resolves came less easily. Alice was dead, and while he recognized that the frontier they'd crossed had provided the United States with its first charitable institution, much was still to be done. He was no longer stung by the thought of changing his relationship to the American School. "I have of late," he wrote, "begun to ponder a good deal on the difficulty of my continuing to be principal."

Thomas wanted the deaf to have the opportunity of secondary education, and he wanted the principal's post at the school to be programmed more fairly. As long as he remained principal rather than, perhaps, advisor—and with Mason Cogswell no longer alive to support him—the board would be unsympathetic and uncooperative. His schedule would be crowded each day; he'd not have time to lobby for higher education; he would never be paid adequately to support his growing family.

In the year ahead, he planned to write books for children. None of the published children's stories in America taught anything of Bible precepts. If deaf boys and girls had been deprived of "knowing," weren't hearing children, too, left partially ignorant? With time, Thomas thought, he could create a new kind of children's book. And if he stepped down as headmaster of the American School, the board of directors might resolve their petty jealousies.

His resolutions had been made. They'd seemed, in spite of some regrets and consternation, to be the right ones. He would always look after the students; now he might help them succeed further. Keeping his plans in mind, he'd submitted his resignation to Daniel Wadsworth and the other board members. If he didn't earn enough writing books or in public speaking, he would add extra tutoring. And if Sophia were willing to put up with him, he'd once more be seeking Solomon's pearl.

Sophia was more than willing. Thomas, she signed and spelled, was loved more by his students as their benefactor than as their headmaster.

The man Thomas picked to replace him at the school was Lewis Weld. Insisting that the board reduce the task load, he also demanded reasonable pay for the job. Any headmaster, he said, must have full authority without having to vie for control with other superintendents. And vacations were mandatory. In his entire thirteen years at the school, his contract had never offered a sabbatical.

Confronted with Thomas' resignation, the very thing they'd connived for, the board of directors was aghast. What would they say to the legislature or Congress? How would the school prevail? Could another headmaster command equal respect? With uncharacteristic humility, the ten board members implored Thomas to contribute, on a permanent basis, the policy opinions they'd once called "impertinent."

Laurent Clerc openly wept on the day that Thomas officially became past principal. The students, beribboned and brass buttoned, had gathered on the lawn, clutching at Thomas as he walked among them. The American School, he'd signed and spelled, was fortunate to bring Mr. Lewis Weld home from Pennsylvania. Mr. Weld would make a fine principal. He had been one of the teachers. As for himself—why, he'd still be coming to the school. He had ideas for the future. The world must be taught the particular gospel that he had learned from Alice Cogswell: that "hearing" could happen through the hands, the mind, the heart, and the soul.

In the six months after his resignation, Thomas was besieged with offers from dozens of institutions across the United States. He was recognized as the very model of that piety and excellence so prized in nineteenth-century society. A minister named Humphrey wrote that no American was "more earnestly sought for so many departments of philanthropic labor." Thomas was asked to be professor or principal at Dartmouth College, New York University, New York High School, and the Oneida Institute. A committee from Boston, Massachusetts, wanted him to initiate the same pioneering work for the blind that he'd performed for the deaf. Connecticut invited him to be the state's first Superintendent of Schools, and Princeton University pressed him to supervise, on campus, the formal training of teachers that he'd outlined in articles and editorials.

He preferred to stay close to Hartford and the American School. Preaching at Center Church, he also worked in town to help organize the country's first teachers' convention, presided over by the famed dictionary maker, Noah Webster. Female education, he preached, was as important as the educating of males. Secondary deaf schools, he urged the convention of teachers, should be an obligation of government.

Articles written by Thomas appeared in the *American Annals of Education, Mother's Magazine,* and the *Connecticut Common School Journal.* Sometimes he wrote of the developing system of American Sign Language, explaining its crossbreeding between the French signs and those continually created by the native deaf of the United States. Yet none of his articles took him as far from his present life as writing his books for children. Cloistered in an upstairs bedroom, Sophia having hushed the children, he conjured up the child he'd once been—outpaced by his more robust companions and curled up in the woods against the trunk of a tree to dream sumptuous dreams of deeds he might do, of books he might read.

The first books he wrote, published by the American Tract Society in New York, were entitled *The Child's Book on the Soul* and *The Child's Book on Repentance.* In rapid succession there followed *The Child's Book of Bible Stories,*

The Youth's Book on Natural Theology, Child's Picture-Defining and Reading Book, Mother's Primer, and *Adam* to *Jonah,* nine volumes of biographies of Bible characters. Collaborating with a Horace Hooker, he would later produce the *Practical Spelling Book* and *The School and Family Dictionary and Illustrative Definer.*

Thomas' books sold almost as well in foreign countries as they did in the United States. The Foreign Missionary Societies used them as English-reading primers, and they were translated into Greek, French, German, Chinese, and Siamese. Eventually, a million copies were circulated—an enormous number for the times—and the well-known educator Henry Barnard wrote how remarkable Thomas was "in bringing the most abstract subjects within grasp" of children.

A letter was delivered to Thomas from the Prince of Siam in Bangkok. "Sir . . ." wrote the prince in stilted English, "I was brave to write you asking you for some certain books. . . . I have now but one of the books which you prepared. It is story of Joseph. . . . Please pardon me if I mistake by unproper word . . . as I am just learning this language, indeed. The Prince T. Y. Chaufa Mong Kut."

In 1837, a prison was built in Hartford and Thomas volunteered to be chaplain. Every Sunday morning, he held prayer service for the prisoners, then walked up the Litchfield Turnpike to the American School. On the pike, the sun pasted shafts of light over the wooden houses and shops, and he felt soothed against a resurgence of the old breathlessness. He was more tired than usual and had written in his diary, "Alas!—how is my energy gone!" But his dreams drove him onward, and if he had to rest in the library of the school, he was soon addressing the children, his hands signing of "that strengthening of faith, that brightening of hope."

The struggles of the deaf to escape their own prisons had sensitized Thomas to all who were shunned and helpless. Besides being chaplain at the jail, he was drawn to similar duties at the newly-built Hartford Retreat for the Insane. In a thirty-two-by-forty-five-foot "preaching room," he saw most of the two hundred patients. Following his first sermon on July 15, 1838, he wrote that "one of the female patients, on account of her incessant loud talking, was led to her room. All the rest were quiet."

Thomas displayed the same calming effect on the mentally ill that he had on the deaf. He viewed the retreat as another uncharted land and talked of the best course being to treat the patients "in a kind manner." After studying the care of patients, he suggested several unique improvements. Never before had regular physical exercise, painting, singing, sewing, and mineral or shell collecting been scheduled at an American sanitorium.

According to Dr. John Butler, superintendent of the retreat, Thomas' skill and friendliness with the patients were extraordinary. On one occasion, Thomas entered a private room to find the male patient poised for attack with a stolen carving knife. Instantly, he took a ring of keys from his pocket, twirling it so that the keys fanned out in a wide circle. "I don't believe you can do this," he said. Fascinated, the patient put down his knife to reach for the keyring.

Another patient once spiraled into a violently manic state, causing the attendants to cower in a hallway. Undaunted, Thomas strode into the room. The patient cursed, picked up a heavy chair, and advanced toward the five-foot-six-inch-tall intruder.

"You wouldn't assault a little man like me?" Thomas asked, whereupon the patient fell to his knees and begged forgiveness.

The attendants at the retreat were astounded by Thomas' powers, but he was unimpressed. It was only a case, he observed, of mutual kinship. The deaf—or the inmates of the prison or the Hartford Retreat—had been society's outcasts. Tormented, they'd existed on the edges of normal life, crippled by mental, emotional, or physical defects. And was he—Thomas—so very different? Hadn't his size and frailty underscored and sometimes restricted the days of his life?

Being alien or "different," he wrote Dr. John Butler, could establish deep ties between people. Possibly all the outcasts adrift in the world longed for their own "upping stones" by which they could be lifted toward lasting salvation.

In 1841, with the remains of some book royalties, Thomas and Sophia rented the Leffingwell house on Prospect Street. Three more children had been born—Catherine Fowler Gallaudet in 1831; Alice Cogswell Gallaudet in 1833; and a final child, Edward Miner Gallaudet, in 1837. The new house was drafty and in need of fixing but had a spare bedroom for overnight guests. Thomas' causes brought a steady assortment of visitors. Black missionaries and white diplomats slept in the guest room. A friend, Alfred Smith, bought a piano for the family.

Thomas seldom spanked the children, though the older

boys might have chosen such swift retribution. Peter Wallace wrote of his "dread of a talk in the study." When he committed his worst childhood mischief, scaring the family's deaf-mute seamstress into thinking a blanket-covered shoe was a rat, Peter's talk with his father sent him from the study to a week in his room with meals of bread and water. No improvised rat ever made another appearance during the family's eight years in the Leffingwell house.

Discipline was balanced with a loving closeness. Little Edward, at age four, crept into Thomas' bed for his early morning geometry lessons. The fifty years separating father from child did not diminish their bond. At the death of a pet rabbit, Edward's tears halted Thomas' research for older son Thomas, Junior, on a Trinity College thesis. Under a sugar maple tree on a hill, the father built a tiny wooden coffin, sharing hammer and nails with his youngest offspring. Bright flowers were picked and a funeral prayer said for the rabbit and its relatives. Ancestors, Thomas said to Edward, were the subject of the research paper in Papa's study. When Edward's tears had dried, he could come listen to the story of his own ancestors, called Huguenots, who fled the country of France in 1685 because they were denied their right to worship.

Children were the linchpin in the union of Thomas and Sophia. At the American School, the students beamed at the mere sight of the former principal. One who "saw" him without seeing was Julia Brace, whom Thomas had recommended to the board for permanent school employment. Sewing, polishing silver, and sorting laundry by smell, Julia was considered indispensable. And in the Leffingwell house, where shelves were stacked with the books he'd written, Thomas continued his home classes for neighborhood children. Daily exercise—the concept he'd pioneered at the Hartford Retreat—had its place on the schedule.

None of the eight Gallaudet children ever made excuses for their mother's lack of hearing. Sophia was an untiring wife, mother, and hostess. Only once did her deafness become a family issue. Eight-year-old Alice had been playing the piano for dinner guests and, wistfully, Sophia signed that she so much missed hearing it. Struck by the realization of the gap in her mother's world, Alice had sobbed her way from the room, vowing never to play "what Mama cannot hear."

Thomas took the child in his arms, with the other children gathering nearby. Music, he said, was beautiful to the deaf. They could feel it in their bodies, sense its rhythms, even if they couldn't hear it with their ears. Many had told him that their silence was a kind of music. Alice must keep on playing the piano—especially for her mama. Someday a cure or treatment might be found for deafness. A special operation. New ear parts invented by scientists or doctors, or ways to increase the volume of sound to deafened ears. Then the hearing who played music would want to have practiced; they'd want to be ready to serenade the deaf. "Yes, Papa," Alice had answered. "You are right. I will play."

By the time Thomas Gallaudet, Jr., worked his way through Trinity College, Alice and Catherine were homespun musicians. Had there been money for lessons, the girls would have chosen to learn cello. But they composed a piano song for their brother's graduation, and on a morning in June, 1842, the family stood on a curb of Main Street to watch Thomas, Junior, march in the Presentation Day Parade. Band music blared and the graduates surged onto the street, a river of black robes. Little Edward, awestruck by the assemblage of people, hopped on one foot in anticipation. The faces he saw beneath graduation caps did not belong to his brother Thomas, but one of them would. Their papa had promised.

When Thomas, Junior, came upon Edward at the curb, he broke pace in his marching to wave and outstretch a hand. Little Edward was invited to join the parade, and the child dove into the double line of woolen robes until even his buoyant grin was barely visible in the stream of black.

The proud father, eyes clearer than usual behind his thick-lensed glasses, looked tenderly at his sons. The firstborn and the last were hand in hand. Fingers, the instruments of sign, were interlaced. The direction of the boys' march seemed to point toward the future, toward years Thomas could not see. Yet in that moment on the curb, in the festive celebrating of knowledge, Thomas signed to Sophia that he felt he *could* see ahead. His own work with the deaf, of bringing them knowing, would not stop with the stopping of his life. The mission of his work would be protected by a broader clasping of hands between his two sons. And whenever those hands parted, to toil elsewhere or to rest, the strictures upon America's deaf might have further loosened their hold.

Chapter
Ten

 The rented Leffingwell house was sold in the winter of 1849, and the Gallaudets had to move. Locating an empty rental, however, would be difficult. Destined to become sole capital of Connecticut in 1875, Hartford was flourishing as a port of entry to the Connecticut River. Its daily newspapers, the *Courant* and the *Times,* served a midcentury population of over 50,000, and the stagecoaches at the Jeremy Addams had been replaced by locomotive trains. The town staked out by Thomas' great-great-great-great grandfather bustled with the manufacture of tools, brushes, woolen goods, paper, firearms, and printed insurance forms.

Thomas combed the south section of town for houses near the Retreat and the American School. An ever-increasing weakness prevented his longer walks, and he admitted in his diary of 1850 that he'd have to yield a bit more to "frailty and mortality." Yet with four of the children gone, the family could occupy much smaller quarters. Thomas,

Junior, already working for the deaf, had founded and become rector of St. Anne's Church for Deaf-Mutes in New York. Peter Wallace was a broker on Wall Street, Sophia a nurse, William an inventor. Jane, who taught at the Hartford School for Girls, and Catherine, Alice, and Edward were still at home.

On Buckingham Street, Thomas came upon a house that halted him in his tracks. He knew Sophia would like the flagstone walk from the gate and, in summer, the well-kept grape arbor and small orchard. Seth Terry, a friend who'd helped Thomas with some decisions at the American School, lived next door. The only drawbacks to the house were the sign reading FOR SALE instead of FOR RENT, and the purchase price of $2,500.00.

Strolling into the yard with Seth Terry to check on the stone-built well, Thomas considered his finances. What he'd saved for the family amounted to just over $2,500.00—but would he be wise to spend it? What if his health failed completely? What if Sophia were left without him? How much could she count on from the royalties from his books?

A week of soul-searching over the house ended in surprise. On the evening of February 22, 1850, Seth Terry delivered a board of directors' report from the American School, casually placing it on the Gallaudets' credenza. Supper was served and eaten before Thomas unsealed the paper. "Whereas, The Rev. Thomas Gallaudet," he read in astonishment, "has rendered many and great services for this institution. . . . Whereas, Soon after he commenced his professional life, at the request of friends of the deaf and dumb, he visited England, Scotland, and France for the purpose of obtaining information as to the best mode of

93

instructing deaf-mutes . . . and Whereas, No pecuniary recompense beyond his actual expenses was ever made to him therefore; and Whereas, Since his connection with this institute was dissolved, he has rendered valuable services for which he has not been compensated; therefore, Voted . . . that the sum of two thousand dollars be appropriated for this purpose. . . ."

Such a sum of money from the board of directors? Thomas was speechless; even his hands lay motionless at his sides as he careened toward Sophia. Seth Terry must have approached the board, but how had he persuaded them? "In all this," Thomas was later to write, "I see the hand of a kind Providence, locking up and reserving this sum for me till I should need it."

On the ninth of April, the family moved into the house on Buckingham Street. Eight days before, at the issuance of the legal deed, five of Thomas' friends surprised him with a "house gift" of $500.00. The bank account stayed intact, and thirteen-year-old Edward and a few neighborhood men carried the smaller furnishings on foot. The covering on Edward's bed, a scripture quilt sewn by women patients at the retreat, was a favorite memento transported by Edward. Hours of his "Bible time" were spent reading the verses on the quilt before sneaking past the parlor Bible to play outdoors.

Surprises abounded when Thomas was invited to an elaborate reunion planned in his honor by his former pupils. Tom Brown, who prepared the invitations, had originated the idea. The response, wrote one former student, ran like "a flame of love . . . a prairie fire through the hearts of the whole deaf-mute band, scattered as they were in various parts of the country."

On September 26, at 2:30 P.M., a procession formed at the American School, proceeding across Hartford to Center Church. Leading the celebrants was Tom Brown, then George Loring, who'd once, as a child, told Thomas, "I love very much Miss Sophia Fowler," and now taught in the school. Fisher Ames Spafford, the acting superintendent of the Ohio School for the Deaf, was next in line. Laurent Clerc walked with principal Lewis Weld and the governor of Connecticut. Teachers and heads of the other state schools were followed by two hundred of Thomas' past pupils, by his family and friends, and by several hundred Hartford citizens.

Chairs filled the sanctuary of Center Church. On the speaker's dais, accompanied by teachers as translators, Tom Brown and Fisher Ames Spafford signed tributes to Thomas. "Thirty-three years ago," said Spafford in American Sign Language, "our ignorance was like chaos. We were without light or hope. . . . There were no educated deaf-mutes sent out into the world; now a large number. . . ."

The applause for Thomas, wryly commented one spectator, was deafening. He was presented with a silver pitcher by his deaf hosts and hostesses, and a duplicate was given to Laurent Clerc. Etched on one side of the pitcher were Thomas and Clerc in Paris, gazing across the ocean to America. On the other side was the American School, surrounded by teachers and pupils, and between the two scenes a likeness of the Abbé Sicard.

Thanking everyone for the reunion, Thomas told his former pupils, "I rejoice to meet you once more." Speaking aloud along with his signing, he said, "Our separation has been long. Some of our number are no more—our beloved

Alice Cogswell. . . . We will cherish her memory."

The audience of Hartford citizens marveled at the sophistication of the deaf men and women. Some of them had found work in factories or were farmers. Others had trained and hoped to be hired as photographers or carpenters. The gap between deafness and hearing was visible only in *the way* language was exchanged. Even so, as the observers could see, hearing people might learn sign—and at least twenty of the deaf participants had been taught by Thomas to vocalize and read lips. Not having heard their own voices, they could nevertheless pronounce understandable sentences. The deaf, said a young Baptist minister, should never have been discarded like empty shells; they were as wondrously designed as any children of the earth.

In the aftermath of buying the house on Buckingham Street and attending the reunion, Thomas' shortness of breath was severe. Morning awakenings were painful through the winter of 1851. Thomas' chest was heavy with phlegm, and the air he inhaled would wheeze and rattle toward his lungs. A doctor prescribed eucalyptus syrup, calling his lifelong symptoms a "constitutional inadequacy." By spring, the taming of cold winds healed better than the eucalyptus, but the summer—dry, hot, and almost windless—left a parched soreness in his chest.

Through June and July, Hartford was hit by such stifling heat that the pace of activities slowed on Main Street. Thomas and Sophia fell sick with dysentery, an infection of the bowel, and were put on semiliquid diets. Within weeks, Sophia had regained her strength, but suddenly sixty-three-year-old Thomas was critically ill. Feeding him juices by spoon, Sophia cooled his forehead with a dampened cloth.

When his regrets had to be sent, in August, to the Convention of Instructors for the Deaf—for which he'd suggested the main topic, "High School Education for the Deaf"—the transcript mailed to him referred to "our father, our teacher, our guide [who] lies ill upon his bed." In the same mail came an honorary degree of Doctor of Laws from Ohio's Western Reserve College for "recognition of his work as promoter of education in many forms."

Friends filled the Buckingham Street house and Thomas, who sometimes was gasping for air, would not dismiss them. "They need to see you as much as me," he told Sophia. "Soon they will need to see you more." Only the doctors called by the family tried his patience. Medicine, he said, could not halt the darkness that would soon be arriving before the dawn. His son Edward wrote later that Thomas was acutely conscious that "the night was coming in which no man can work."

On Wednesday, September 10, sometime near a sweltering noon, he lay on the open sheets of his bed while daughter Sophia fanned him. A silence beyond words and sound was slowly descending. A shaft of sunlight edged past the window shade onto the rug. Thomas' face strained with the effort at breath, but he whispered of feeling as if he were being ushered onto one of the old stagecoaches—the black carriage smelling of leather and polish, swaying him past Sophia, who held out her arms, and past his children to a new and unending path. The journey must be made. Books of wisdom filled his traveling trunks, and in the distance he saw Hartford's Main Street stretch onto Little River Bridge.

Smiling, Thomas opened his eyes and touched the tips of

his daughter's fingers. No one else of the family was in the room. Murmuring then that he had been made content, he turned over on the wrinkled sheet with the words, "I will go to sleep." The fanning continued, heat pressed away from his pillow, but not until another doctor arrived to examine the patient did it become obvious that Thomas' sleep was eternal.

By sundown, the news had spread across Hartford, and Buckingham Street was filling with townspeople and with students and faculty from the American School. Deaf and hearing alike thronged at the Gallaudets' gate, tears coursing down faces. As the twilight deepened, mourners spontaneously sang a hymn that Thomas himself had written in 1848. "Ever near Oh! Jesus be," the voices chanted in sorrow, "With thy grace to succor me, lest I stray away from thee; leave, ah! leave me not alone. . . ."

Among the shadows, the chorus was joined by the music of hands. The deaf, too, had memorized Thomas' hymn. Patiently, he had taught them to fill their emptiness with the shape and meaning of words. "Till the struggling race is run," signed the deaf children from the American School, hands speaking in love to their benefactor. "Till the fight of faith is done, and the Crown of Victory won, leave, ah! leave me not alone. . . ."

Thomas' funeral was held at South Congregational Church, Center Church having been temporarily closed for repairs. A crowd of thousands listened to eulogies by Laurent Clerc and by Dr. Harvey Prindle Peet, principal of the New York Institute for the Deaf. The cortege to Cedar Hill Cemetery, led by a black-veiled Sophia and the family, drew

Thomas' friends from various religious denominations. A Father Brady of Hartford incurred the censure of his Catholic superiors rather than miss the Protestant ceremony.

Over the next months, tributes to Thomas appeared in journals and magazines; his name was honored by educational institutions and philanthropic societies, and his diaries and letters were donated to the archives at Yale. People, some from the Hartford Retreat and some from offices of government, wrote Sophia that they'd heard Thomas speak at a prayer service, a meeting, a school, a church, and had never forgotten him. The deaf who'd planned his reunion formed an association, headed by Laurent Clerc, to erect a memorial on the grounds of the American School. In 1854, three years after Thomas' death, an engraved marble and granite structure, designed and sculpted by two deaf-mute artists, was unveiled at the school.

Thomas, Junior, remained rector of St. Anne's Church in New York, and the other children, now grown, pursued their professions and interests. Edward, nearly sixteen, was the one at a loss over what he would become or how to honor his father. He was dissatisfied with his bank job and switched to part-time teaching at the American School, enrolling also in Trinity College. At his graduation, his brother Thomas came to the Presentation Day Parade. This time, Thomas, Junior, stood on the curb and Edward, hand outstretched, marched in black robe and cap.

Launched into full-time teaching, Edward Miner Gallaudet began to pursue his father's goal of higher education for the deaf. Only twenty years old, he was offered a superintendent's post at a new elementary school for the deaf and blind in Washington, D.C. Amos Kendall, a philanthropist,

99

was donating several acres of his private estate for the school. Edward accepted the offer on the condition that students be permitted instruction past any four-year limit. Left to his own devices, he intended to bring high school and college level learning within the grasp of the deaf.

The new school, called Columbia Institution, opened in 1857 and was at first privately supported. It consisted of two ramshackle dormitories. From the upper windows was a view of the domeless capital building and of a grassy commons between unpaved streets. By 1864, a two-and-a-half-story brick building had been erected. Seven deaf boys completed their preparatory requirements for college. Sophia—who was to live almost to the age of eighty—was school matron. The country was beset by civil war, but President Abraham Lincoln studied and signed a congressional bill instigated by Edward. Columbia Institution was authorized to confer collegiate degrees and to change its name to National Deaf-Mute College.

In 1887, women were admitted to the growing institution, and a government grant provided additional buildings. Edward, appointed president, had traveled to Europe in 1867 on a leave of absence to retrace his father's journey. Like Thomas, he'd visited schools in England, Scotland, and France. And like his father, he approved a "combined system" of education. Sign, he said, *was* the natural language of the deaf, but early oral training could develop useful lipreading and vocal skills.

The long debate over the oral and silent systems was, however, not so easily resolved. In 1880, the International Conference of Teachers of the Deaf had met in Milan, Italy, passing a resolution favoring the Pure Oral Method. Sign language, except in the United States, was once more disparaged. Teachers admitted that "no Pure Oralist could effectively instruct a class of more than ten children," yet oral language won the vote because it would have to be learned only by the deaf, not the hearing.

In America, a few supporters of Pure Oralism campaigned for schools. Horace Mann, first secretary of the Massachusetts School Board, and Samuel Gridley Howe, director of the Massachusetts School for the Blind, petitioned the General Court of that state for subsidies. Their petition failed, but Massachusetts eventually had its oral Clarke School for the Deaf and its Horace Mann School, and Alexander Graham Bell, inventor of the telephone, supported the Pure Oral Method. Bell and Edward Miner Gallaudet came to symbolize the oral-silent war—with Bell wanting to merge deaf children into society by obliterating sign language and Edward arguing that sign gave the deaf a valid language of their own that freed them from having to learn and speak in words they couldn't hear.

Whatever the opinions on oral versus silent method, the deaf were gaining wider recognition across the United States. In 1880, the National Association of the Deaf (NAD) formed in Cincinnati, Ohio. Among other projects, it succeeded in having Civil Service examinations adapted for deaf applicants. By 1901, the National Fraternal Society of the Deaf (NFSD) was founded in Flint, Michigan, to offer insurance to deaf clients. Today, the NFSD is one of the nation's fifteen largest insurance firms.

The first half of the twentieth century not only inspired the deaf to dream as Thomas dreamed of "what *might* be," but saw many dreams become fact. Thomas had told his daughter Alice that sound might someday be made louder for deafened ears, and in 1900 Dr. Ferdinand Alt of Vienna invented the first hearing aid. Dry-cell batteries, a microphone, and a receiver amplified sound for ears that had less than profound deafness, enabling some of the deaf to suddenly hear in varying degrees. By the 1940s, ten-inch-high battery aids were worn in chest harnesses, and group hearing aids for classrooms used a microphone for the teacher, aids for the students, and receiving coils on the floor. By the middle of the twentieth century, ear units were effective in galvanizing the "residual hearing" of the partially deaf, and the exploding transistor revolution produced aids tiny enough to be barely visible when worn.

In 1926, the audiometer was invented in the United States. Sounds of measured pitches and volumes, transmitted through earphones, permitted a measured test of hearing response. With audiometers, hundreds of thousands of unsuspected hearing losses were uncovered. Many children performing poorly in school were found to be hearing-impaired. Some, misdiagnosed as mentally retarded, were rediagnosed as virtually deaf—and some, who'd been thought totally deaf, showed on audiometers that they possessed residual hearing. Twentieth-century advances in medicine could send these children to *otologists,* medical specialists who test further for deafness. Otologists are able to treat ear infections with antibiotic drugs and perform new surgeries to correct specific abnormalities or injuries to the ear.

In the last twenty years, hearing impairment has been the subject of worldwide investigation by physicians, social workers, speech therapists, sociologists, psychologists, and psychiatrists. Detection of hearing loss in newborn infants has become possible, and treatment is often given in hospitals and clinics. Immunization of females protects against German measles, or *rubella*, which has been discovered to be a leading cause of fetal deafness.

Group intelligence tests administered to deaf and hearing children point to what both Dr. Mason Cogswell and Thomas believed: that the deaf are deficient in environmental stimulation, not intellectual capacity. Jean Piaget, a twentieth-century Swiss psychologist, determined that deaf children develop individual forms of thought even without acquiring language. Words, said Piaget, are the product and not the origin of early thought.

In American schools, mainstreaming and specialized guidance of the deaf into regular classrooms has helped to normalize a deaf child's environment. Mainstreaming became popular in the early 1970s when the combined system first urged by Thomas was renamed Total Communication. Sign, lipreading, and vocal speech were finally taught together. Over the years, sign itself has evolved into a more complex and structured language. American Sign Language, sometimes called Ameslan, is now most freely used among deaf conversationalists. However, "sign English"—the forming of standard ASL signs in the precise word order of English—can make speech between deaf and hearing easier.

In 1968, President Lyndon Johnson approved legislation to give financial assistance to America's handicapped. Five years later, the 1973 Rehabilitation Act protected the handicapped from job discrimination and required organizations receiving federal funds to provide sign interpreters for the deaf. Public Law 94-142, passed in 1975, grants economic aid for all handicapped children who need education in specialized facilities.

The greater social awareness of the twentieth century has greatly benefited the profoundly and partially deaf. The National Technical Institute for the Deaf in Rochester, New York, confers Ph.D.'s in technical subjects. The cities of St. Paul, Seattle, and New Orleans have junior college centers for deaf students, and programs operate at California State University at Northridge. In the mid-nineteenth century, the deaf were hired, if they were hired at all, to sew, print, or farm, but deaf men and women are currently active as teachers, authors, lawyers, dancers, artists, actors, chemists, veterinarians, computer programmers, mechanical engineers, accountants, systems analysts, and medical technicians. In 1977, the first deaf-born lawyer graduated to fanfare at the Massachusetts Institute of Technology; in February, 1982, a deaf lawyer submitted an unprecedented petition, still pending, to the United States Supreme Court to install special electronic lipreading scanners that would allow him to argue a case.

Deaf children and adults in the 1980s can participate in local or long-distance telephone conversations with two-way teletypewriters (TTY's or TDD's) that type vocalized words onto paper or transpose them into print on attached word screens. The deaf can read vocalization on an increasing number of participating television shows by hooking up to their sets "closed caption convertors" that translate spoken-aloud language into the kind of subtitles seen in foreign films. The year 1981 brought the subject of deafness to public acclaim through the award-winning Broadway play, *Children of a Lesser God,* the story of a speech therapist and his deaf pupil. The play's popularity prompted numerous business seminars, political action groups, hearing schools, and public libraries to provide sign interpreters or classes in sign instruction. And in this same year, doctors reported the partial success of cochlear implant surgery—a replacing of bone in the inner ear with electrodes that have, so far, transmitted loud sounds to several hundred deaf patients.

From the day that Thomas Gallaudet met a little deaf girl named Alice Cogswell, he strove to gain for the deaf their rightful place in society. He was especially compelled toward those children who longed to learn and know. Today, National Deaf-Mute College, supervised by Edward until his death in 1917, bears its final name in Thomas' honor, Gallaudet College. Spread over ninety-three acres in Washington, D.C., the college is the only liberal arts institution for the deaf in the world. Its student body of over 1,500 comes from every state in the union, from eight provinces of Canada, and twenty-two foreign countries. A program of Total Communication blends the oral and silent methods of teaching on a campus that accommodates a preschool, elementary school, high school, and graduate and continuing education facility for adults. Through the International Center of Deafness, the college initiates and strengthens programs for the deaf in various nations; its Edward Miner Gallaudet Library holds the world's largest collection of books, periodicals, and films about deafness.

On the grounds of Gallaudet College and at the American School is a bronze statue that was commissioned from Daniel Chester French, famed American sculptor. The statue, engraved with the words FRIEND, BENEFACTOR, TEACHER, depicts Thomas seated in a chair with nine-year old Alice Cogswell beside him. With his right hand,

Thomas is showing Alice how to form the letter *A* of the manual alphabet. The deaf-mute child, face upturned in affection and wonder, is learning a remarkable means by which to listen and speak.

Surveys in the United States put present-day figures of the hearing-handicapped at nearly twenty million, including at least two million profoundly deaf—those once referred to as "deaf and dumb." But to Thomas, accusations of "dumb" or "dummy" were inappropriate for deafness. He dreamed that the deaf would find pride within themselves and create their own cultural heritage in the richness of sign. Because of his work with Alice Cogswell and hundreds of other children—work that was carried on by the oldest and the youngest of his sons—deafness today is far less of a handicap making people different than a human characteristic making them distinct. For the deaf of the twentieth century, enrichment is possible through modern medicine, government, and technology, as well as through social research and language that bring expanding opportunities to achieve.

The nineteenth-century essayist Ralph Waldo Emerson wrote that "an institution is the lengthened shadow of one man." Thomas Gallaudet's legacy of knowledge and communication for the nonhearing extended far beyond even his own personal mission. The shadows cast by the American School and Gallaudet College are larger than the mightiest dreams of the eager boy from Hartford, Connecticut, who yearned throughout childhood to overcome his frailties and persevere.

Bibliography

BENDER, RUTH E. *The Conquest of Deafness.* Cleveland and London: The Press of Case Western Reserve University, 1970.

BENDERLY, BERYL LIEFF. *Dancing Without Music.* New York: Doubleday, Anchor Press, 1980.

DE GERING, ETTA. *Gallaudet, Friend of the Deaf.* New York: David McKay Co., Inc., 1964.

"Gallaudet and the Difference of Deafness." *The Washington Magazine,* October, 1978.

Gallaudet College. "Careers in Deafness." Public Service Programs. Washington, D.C.

Gallaudet College. "PL 94-142 and Deaf Children." *Gallaudet Alumni Newsletter,* Fall 1977.

Gallaudet College. *Gallaudet Today,* Fall 1979.

GALAUDET, EDWARD M. *Life of Thomas Hopkins Gallaudet.* New York: Henry Holt & Co., 1888.

Diaries of Thomas Hopkins Gallaudet. Washington, D.C.: Library of Congress.

Letters and Journals of Thomas Hopkins Gallaudet. New Haven, Connecticut: Yale University Archives.

GANNON, JACK. *Deaf Heritage—A Narrative History of Deaf America.* Silver Spring, Maryland: National Association for the Deaf, 1980.

GREENBERG, JOANNE. *In This Sign.* New York: Holt, Rinehart and Winston, 1970.

MERRILL, EDWARD C. "Universal Rights and Progress in Education of the Deaf." Washington, D.C.: Gallaudet College.

O'ROURKE, T. J. *A Basic Course in Manual Communication.* Silver Spring, Maryland: National Association of the Deaf, 1973.

SPRADLEY, THOMAS S. AND JAMES P. *Deaf Like Me.* New York: Random House, 1978.

STERNBERG, MARTIN. *American Sign Language: A Comprehensive Dictionary.* New York: Harper & Row, 1981.

WEVER, E. G. *Theory of Hearing.* New York: John Wiley & Sons, 1945.

WOODS, W. H., SR. *The Forgotten People.* St. Petersburg, Florida: Dixie Press.

WRIGHT, DAVID. *Deafness.* New York: Stein & Day, 1969.

National
Service Organizations
and Centers for the Deaf

GALLAUDET COLLEGE ALUMNI ASSOCIATION
Gallaudet College
Washington, D.C. 20002

Publication: *Gallaudet Alumni Newsletter*

ALEXANDER GRAHAM BELL ASSOCIATION FOR THE
DEAF, INC.
3417 Volta Place, N.W.
Washington, D.C. 20007

Publications: *Volta Review, Newsounds*

HELEN KELLER NATIONAL CENTER FOR DEAF-BLIND
YOUTHS AND ADULTS
111 Middle Neck Road
Sands Point, New York 11050

Publication: *The Nat-Cent News*

NATIONAL ASSOCIATION OF THE DEAF
814 Thayer Avenue
Silver Spring, Maryland 20910

Publications: *The Broadcaster, The Deaf American*

JUNIOR NATIONAL ASSOCIATION OF THE DEAF
138 Key Parkway
Frederick, Maryland 21701

Publication: *Junior Deaf American*

NATIONAL THEATRE OF THE DEAF
305 Great Neck Road
Waterford, Connecticut 06385

NATIONAL CENTER FOR LAW AND THE HANDICAPPED
University of Notre Dame
Notre Dame, Indiana 46556

Publication: *Amicus*

AMERICAN ATHLETIC ASSOCIATION OF THE DEAF
3916 Lantern Drive
Silver Spring, Maryland 20902

Publication: *AAAD Bulletin*

EPISCOPAL CONFERENCE OF THE DEAF
429 Somerset Avenue
St. Louis, Missouri 63119

Publication: *The Deaf Episcopalian*

NATIONAL CONGRESS OF JEWISH DEAF
9102 Edmonston Court
Greenbelt, Maryland 20770

Publication: *NCJD Quarterly*

NATIONAL CATHOLIC OFFICE FOR THE DEAF
Trinity College
Washington, D.C. 20016

Publication: *Listening*

INTERNATIONAL LUTHERAN DEAF ASSOCIATION
500 North Broadway
St. Louis, Missouri 63102

Publication: *The Deaf Lutheran*

NATIONAL FRATERNAL SOCIETY OF THE DEAF
1300 W. Northwest Highway
Mt. Prospect, Illinois 60056

Publication: *The Frat*

NATIONAL TECHNICAL INSTITUTE FOR THE DEAF
ALUMNI PROGRAMS
1 Lomb Memorial Drive
Rochester, New York 14623

Publication: *NTID Alumni Newsletter*

Index

ABOUT THE AUTHOR

Anne E. Neimark was born in Chicago and attended Bryn Mawr College in Pennsylvania. She has written over two hundred stories and articles as well as several biographies for young readers. *Touch of Light, the Story of Louis Braille* won first prize for juvenile literature from the Friends of American Writers. Her other books include *Sigmund Freud, the World Within; With This Gift, the Story of Edgar Cayce;* and *Damien, the Leper Priest.*

Mrs. Neimark is married and has three children. At present, she lives in Highland Park, Illinois.